# Museum Trusteeship

## BY ALAN D. ULLBERG, WITH PATRICIA ULLBERG

AMERICAN ASSOCIATION OF MUSEUMS

WASHINGTON, D.C.

1981

Designed by Julian Waters,
Bookmark Studio, Washington, D.C.

# Table of Contents

## III  Structure and Operation of the Board   34

## IV Accountability of Museum Trustees 62

## V Liabilities of Museum Trustees 73

## Further Readings 93
## Index 118

# Foreword

A handbook for museum trustees has been a concern of the Trustee Committee of the American Association of Museums for many years. Plans for this book began in response to the need, strongly expressed by museum trustees, for a clearer definition of trustee responsibility, accountability and liability in today's climate and for specific guidelines to help trustees in carrying out their obligations. It was felt, too, that such a handbook, the first of its kind for museum trustees, would clarify for museum staff and the interested public the role of museum trustees in a changing society.

In 1978 the chairman of the Trustee Committee, Esther D. Anderson, in consultation with its vice-chairman for publications, Katharine S. White, appointed a committee to supervise the preparation and production of a handbook addressed to museum trustees. Those appointed were selected for the length of their museum service as well as for the various sizes and disciplines of the organizations they represented. They included:

KATHARINE S. WHITE (chairman), Trustee, Museum of Fine Arts, Boston; Vice-Chairman for Publications of the AAM Trustee Committee

WILLIAM T. ALDERSON, Director of Museum Studies and Art Conservation, University of Delaware; former Director of the American Association for State and Local History; member of the AAM Committee on Ethics; former Chairman of the AAM Accreditation Commission

MARGOT C. LINDSAY, Trustee, Museum of Fine Arts, Boston; author of *A Handbook for Citizen Boards and Councils* (1977)

WILLIAM G. SWARTCHILD, JR., Chairman of the Board of Trustees, Field Museum of Natural History; Midwest Regional Representative of the AAM Trustee Committee; member of the AAM Committee on Ethics

CHARLES VAN RAVENSWAAY, Director Emeritus, Henry Francis duPont Winterthur Museum; former member of the AAM Council; former AAM President

JAMES M. WALTON, President of the Board of Trustees, Carnegie Institute

ESTHER D. ANDERSON (ex officio), Vice-President of the Museum of Fine Arts, Boston; Chairman of the AAM Trustee Committee; Chairman of the AAM Legislative Committee.

The committee's tenure was saddened by the death in the fall of 1980 of one of its original members, George W. Passage, president of the War Memorial Museum, chairman of the board of the Mariners Museum of Newport News and editor of the *Newport News Times Herald*.

In the spring of 1978 the Handbook Committee and the Executive Committee of the AAM Trustee Committee, after considering possible authors, asked Alan D. Ullberg to prepare the handbook for museum trustees. Ullberg, an authority on U.S. law for museums and the associate general counsel of the Smithsonian Institution, is an associate professorial lecturer in art administration at George Washington University and is, with Patricia Ullberg, working on a book on conflicts of interest in museums. He was also a member of the drafting committee that prepared *Museum Ethics*, published by the AAM in 1978, and served as the book's technical editor. His coauthor in preparing the trustee handbook was Patricia Ullberg, a Washington writer and artist. Robert C. Lind, Jr., Esq., who has specialized in conflicts of interest and trusteeship questions, completed the writing team.

The undertaking was approved by the AAM Executive Committee in September 1978, and work commenced. Over the next three years the Handbook Committee, in several extended sessions, reviewed and revised the outlines and drafts prepared by Mr. Ullberg and his associates.

The research, writing and publication of *Museum Trusteeship* were made possible by the generous response of:

George Gund Foundation, Cleveland
Tosco Corporation, Los Angeles
Brown Foundation, Houston

Merrimack Valley Textile Museum, North Andover, Mass.
Moody Foundation, Galveston
Time, Inc., New York
Fisher Charitable Trust, Pittsburgh.
We acknowledge their support, and the additional assistance of
Mr. and Mrs. Jacob Gitelman and Mrs. Mary Louise Wilding-
White, with sincere appreciation.

We gratefully acknowledge, too, the assistance of Lawrence L.
Reger, AAM director; the AAM program staff, particularly Jane
W. North, trustee coordinator, and Pamela Johnson, assistant
director for programs; the AAM publications staff, especially Ellen
Cochran Hicks, editor of publications; Ann Hofstra Grogg, the
book's editor and production manager; and Julian Waters, the
book's designer. We appreciate, too, the thoughtful and careful
attention that the author and his talented associates gave to our
many concerns and questions.

This book is offered in the hope that it will provide an opportunity for museum trustees to share the challenges they
experience as volunteer members of museum governing boards,
a unique American institution whose value we all cherish. We
have tried to point out some of the problems trustees face and
to offer some possible solutions. We suggest standards that we
hope trustees can achieve, but they should not be discouraged
from this effort if implementation takes time.

Museums and their trustees have not escaped the public
scrutiny of the litigious age in which we live, but the number of
actual lawsuits brought against them is still relatively small. We
describe some of these cases in detail because they are important
and clearly indicate current trends. We also point out the protective measures that are available.

Museum trusteeship is a complex and demanding service.
Museums are widely different and constantly evolving, and their
trustees' duties and procedures vary accordingly. Hence the
Handbook Committee did not find the task an easy one. As a
group we did not always agree, but the compromise of viewpoints
we achieved has made the book stronger and, we hope, more
valuable in the end. We did share a desire to fulfill our mandate:
to present as comprehensive a working manual as possible on

the current responsibilities, accountability and liabilities of museum trustees.

I enjoyed chairing this committee and appreciated its competence and commitment. We urge you to give your most serious consideration to the text that follows. We hope it will prove helpful, and we expect it will stimulate discussion.

KATHARINE S. WHITE
Handbook Committee Chairman

# Preface

The authors have attempted to outline the major responsibilities of museum trustees and to relate those duties to the potential for legal liability if they are neglected. We have sought not to dwell on liabilities, for trusteeship should be a satisfying and fulfilling service, performed with confidence and optimism. Our objective has been to offer some guidance for the protection of trustees in those areas that can become a cause for concern.

The text is intended for trustees rather than lawyers and purposely avoids technical legal terminology. This approach has been possible because of the efforts of Patricia Ullberg, a writer, to state plainly the essence of complex legal concepts propounded by Alan Ullberg, a museum attorney. For the authors, the handbook represents a culmination of years of collaborative writing on museum topics.

The legal underpinning of the book and the section listing further references are the work of Robert C. Lind, Jr. Mr. Lind, who began working with us while a law student, is now an associate professor of law at Southwestern University School of Law. He has given the handbook the benefit of his research and supportive criticism, based upon his comprehensive understanding of trusts, nonprofit corporations and museums. Attorneys who use this volume will find the references of great value in fashioning solutions to questions their clients may have about their museum board service.

We are grateful to our many colleagues in law and in museums who provided information and advice on the legal and administrative aspects of museums and trusteeship. Their assistance has been invaluable in preparing and verifying this text.

We were fortunate to have the assistance of Ann Hofstra Grogg, an editor skillful in organizing the many concerns of the book into a coherent and readable text. Without her hard work, patience and good humor, our task as authors would have been more difficult and much less enjoyable.

We salute the Handbook Committee, a body remarkable not only for its collective experience and knowledge but also for the ability to submerge individual opinions in the interest of reaching a consensus on the dozens of points in this volume about which reasonable men and women can differ.

ALAN D. ULLBERG
PATRICIA ULLBERG

# Introduction
# to Trusteeship

Those who have been chosen to serve on the governing boards of American museums have a singular opportunity to direct the keeping of our nation's irreplaceable cultural and natural heritage. In their role as policy makers, museum trustees influence the course of their institution's present and future mission. Theirs is an important charge and a rewarding service.

The purpose of this handbook is to provide a convenient summary of the custodial, legal and ethical obligations of museum trustees. It comes at this particular time because museums are experiencing many changes. Attendance is up dramatically, for museums have a new visibility as important centers of cultural life. There is also heightened awareness of the role of the nonprofit organization in the economy, and greater public and media interest in the performance of the volunteer boards that manage nonprofit organizations. Museum governing boards are, therefore, subject to increased public scrutiny. At the same time, museums have been receiving more revenue in the form of government grants that carry with them demands for accountability and compliance with federal laws and regulations. Finally, as museum programs and operations expand, their management becomes increasingly complex.

It is important that museum trustees keep up with these changes in museum operations, in public attitudes and in legislation and that they are prepared to meet the increasing demands and challenges of their position. Even experienced trustees may find that they are unfamiliar with current trends. This handbook is intended for them as well as for new trustees, who will find the guidelines summarized here helpful in orienting them to their functions and responsibilities.

After a brief introduction to trusteeship, this handbook will consider the specific duties of museum trustees as policy makers and overseers, the structure and operation of the museum board, the entities to which museum trustees are accountable and the legal liabilities of trustees. References for further reading, keyed to each topic as it is considered, are listed at the conclusion of the text. The American Association of Museums hopes that the information presented here will assist all museum trustees not only in enhancing their own effectiveness and that of their museums but in gaining added personal satisfaction from challenges well met and jobs well done.

# ꙰꙰꙰꙰꙰꙰꙰꙰꙰꙰꙰ *Museums*

The American Association of Museums defines museums as nonprofit organizations dedicated to the collecting, preservation, study, display and educational use of objects. They are established as permanent institutions so the objects in their care may be ensured responsible stewardship. They are open to the public on some regular schedule. For the purposes of this handbook, the term "museum" encompasses not only traditional collecting institutions, such as art, history and science museums, zoos, aquariums and herbariums, but also nonprofit organizations that exhibit but do not own objects, such as planetariums, art centers and science and technology centers. The trustees of related nonprofit organizations, such as libraries, archives and historical societies, will also find this handbook useful in their roles.

All these organizations fall within the broad legal definition of public charity. Most museums function under some type of a board that sets policy, oversees the operations of the institution and ensures that it is well managed and true to its purpose. Government museums may have dual direction, being administered in part by a unit or agency of government and in part by a board. Their trustees must be particularly well informed of the scope of their responsibilities, understanding how authority and responsibility are divided between the governmental unit and the board. But the boards of all museums and related organizations share the same concerns and problems. The difference in scale between the small and the large museum does not mean that the trustees of the former are any less accountable or liable for their actions than the trustees of the latter, though trustees of the small museum may be less visible.

## ᓚᓚᓚᓚᓚᓚᓚᓚᓚᓚᓚᓚᓚᓚ **Trustees**

Though they are sometimes called governors, regents, directors or commissioners, the board members of the types of nonprofit cultural organizations dealt with in this handbook are generally referred to as trustees. The term is apt, reflecting semantically the standard of care to which such board members may be held. Trustees owe a duty of disinterested loyalty to an organization *supported by* that has an avowedly eleemosynary purpose; the public welfare *charity.* is their charge. All museum trustees are subject to the same basic obligations: they are private individuals who, as a body, hold their institution's assets in trust as fiduciaries for the public.

Under the law, a fiduciary is an individual entrusted to carry out certain duties for another, who may be incapable of carrying out those duties for himself. That other can be a single individual, a group, the general public or some specified segment thereof. In all matters concerning the trust, the trustee-fiduciary must put his* own interests aside and act with absolute loyalty to the beneficiary, the person or group for which he exercises his trust. This obligation is not merely a passive commitment; it is not enough for the fiduciary to prevent harm to the object of the trust. The obligation is, rather, an active mandate to promote the interests of the beneficiary with all the means and skills at his disposal. The museum trustee's ultimate responsibility to his museum is to ensure through his active and affirmative guidance that his institution's resources are prudently and efficiently managed to serve its purposes.

The law imposes liability upon the trustee if he fails in the fulfillment of his obligation. Although the comparison may seem startling outside the legal context, the status of trusteeship in law is like that of marriage. Both are conditions entered into voluntarily

* In the text of this handbook, "he" and related pronouns are used in the generic sense to denote the person, male or female.

that nonetheless automatically and immediately confer upon the individual binding legal and ethical obligations prescribed by law and custom, regardless of whether those obligations are understood. Consent is implicit with acceptance. This condition is the direct opposite of a business contract, in which one party is bound only to definite terms and has rights as agreed upon by both parties. Because the terms of trusteeship are not spelled out in contract form, it is imperative that those consenting to join museum boards are fully aware of the accountability and liabilities inherent in the status they voluntarily assume.

## ㄹㄹㄹㄹㄹㄹ Historical Precedents

Justice Oliver Wendell Holmes once said that a page of history is worth a volume of logic. A brief review of trusteeship and the trust in historical perspective may give today's board member a clearer understanding of his status and current ethical and legal responsibilities.

Precedents for trust or fiduciary relationships are found in Judaic law, which recognized charity as a religious duty, and in Egyptian and Sumerian law, which encouraged charitable trusts for religious reasons. King Hammurabi's law code in the second millennium B.C. specifically recognized trusts as the holding of property by one individual for another and prescribed legal remedies for abuse or betrayal. Hellenic Greek and, later, Roman law brought the concept of the charitable trust closer to the modern definition of philanthropy. Roman law allowed property or funds to be set aside for charitable purposes, for the use of "living legal heirs." As inherited and transmitted by Christianity, the concept of the trust continued to have a strong moral basis.

The immediate historical antecedent of the modern eleemosynary or philanthropic organization was the medieval beneficence. As a bequest to the church to be administered for "pious causes," the beneficence could be established for the relief of suffering on earth. Gifts and legacies could be earmarked for general public welfare, such as the upkeep and repair of hospitals and roads. Enforcement of these bequests was originally the province of ecclesiastical courts, but secular courts gradually assumed jurisdiction. The Statute of Charitable Uses passed by Parliament in 1601 recognized a variety of charitable purposes, established that property devoted to such uses was outside the taxing powers of the Crown and provided a mechanism for ensuring that the property was properly managed by those entrusted with its administration or control. Although the attorney general retained power to enforce charities for the common good, the power to oversee or investigate charities was usually carried out by commissions either existing under legislative authority or appointed by a court of equity. Enforcement of charitable "uses" or trusts remained under the ultimate jurisdiction of the courts, however, and the principle became firmly established that all charities function subject to the power of the courts to give direction whenever necessary. Court action could be initiated upon petition by the attorney general or other official or individual with an interest in the operation of the charity.

Today all organizations legally defined as public charities, and that includes museums, remain subject to court intervention. Charitable purposes presume that the entity carries out an activity for the public benefit, and the standards for its conduct are those for a public activity.

For the past hundred years, however, the prevailing legal structure for museums and related organizations has not been that of the common law charitable trust but that of an artificial entity, called the corporation, created under legislation to exist in perpetuity and with sufficient powers to accomplish its purposes. The common law trust can be created by an individual in his will or by other means evidencing his intent to set his property aside and have it used for certain purposes. In the 17th and 18th centuries business corporations were chartered by specific acts of Parliament. In the new United States they were chartered by state legislatures. The Massachusetts Historical Society was chartered by a special act of the Massachusetts legislature in the late 18th century, and during the 19th and early 20th centuries many museums were chartered by legislative action.

In the 19th century state legislatures also passed "enabling statutes" to facilitate the formation of business corporations by allowing them to be created by individuals and groups without a specific legislative charter so long as they conformed to the outlines of the enabling legislation. Some charitable organizations were created under business corporation statutes, though many others continued to be chartered by special legislation. The proliferation of nonprofit corporations in recent decades led to the development of the Model Nonprofit Corporation Act, drafted in the 1950s by the American Bar Association to serve as a standard for achieving uniformity in state nonprofit corporation enabling statues. Most states now have a separate set of laws for the organization and operation of the nonprofit corporation.

Whether an organization is a charitable trust or a nonprofit corporation, its purposes are the same—to carry out publicly approved charitable objectives such as education or the promotion of the public welfare—and its board members are fiduciaries. There may be legal argument about the precise standard of care the trustees of a nonprofit corporation are required to maintain and whether all the technical rules pertaining to the charitable trust are applicable. But since it has been clearly established that the directors of a business corporation are fiduciaries for the economic interests of the entity and its stockholders, use of the corporate mode for nonprofit organizations does not negate the board members' status as fiduciaries.

The phenomenon of charitable trusteeship, by which groups of private individuals voluntarily assume the governance of an organization with public purposes and thereby accept legal responsibility for that entity despite their volunteer status, is the prevalent mode of organization only in England and in countries that have inherited English common law, such as the United States. The network of charitable organizations is not so well developed in other countries, where education and social welfare remain the province of government. Museums in these countries are units of government, organized and operated as subunits or departments. Consequently they can be subject not only to political influence but to competing claims on government resources.

Responsible trusteeship contributes to the pluralism so highly prized in the United States. Even in government museums the boards of trustees, often called commissioners, assure participation by private citizens. In all nonprofit organizations the bargain struck between charities and the English Crown centuries ago—relief from taxation and other prerogatives of the Crown in exchange for attending to the public welfare—still holds. But if trusteeship is not responsibly performed, the government can intervene and assume control.

The museum trustee has the honor of community recognition. He has the chance to contribute actively to his community's cultural life and to the advancement of knowledge and education in general. He can exercise and develop new skills. At the same time, museum trusteeship is a complex and demanding service. To perform it successfully, trustees must have a full understanding of their responsibilities, accountability and liabilities. These are the subjects of the following chapters.

# II Responsibilities of Museum Trustees

**M**useum trustees make policy for the museum and monitor the execution of that policy. The board is ultimately responsible for every aspect of the museum—its collections, its physical plant, its finances, its personnel and all its operations, activities and programs.

This chapter will discuss the full scope of the board's charge and offer suggestions for formulating and implementing policy with regard to its responsibilities. Specifically, these include clarifying the goals and purpose of the institution, planning for its future, ensuring continued tax-exempt status and compliance with regulatory laws, and formulating policies for managing and using the collections and the physical plant. Providing for the management and augmentation of finances, including budgeting, fund raising and auditing, are also basic board tasks. The board must see to it that a personnel policy is enacted and implemented and that it meets legal standards and provides for equitable treatment of staff. Finally, the board has a responsibility for evaluation; it has to review all aspects of the museum's operations and programs to assess how well they fulfill stated goals and policies.

## General Policy Making

The governing board is the museum's guiding force; it determines the present and future direction of the museum. The trustee's most valuable contribution to his institution is the wisdom and perspective he brings to planning goals and formulating policies and to monitoring their application. Like the boards of other charitable entities, the museum board is typically made up of individuals representing a broad spectrum of background and experience who are united by a strong commitment to the institution. Although few museum board members are trained in museum work, they direct the operation of an institution staffed by museum professionals in an example of control by a board of laymen of a function that is specialized in many of its operations.

## POLICY AND ADMINISTRATION

The trustees are ultimately responsible for the success of the museum's programs but must remain aloof from the actual execution of those programs, which is properly the responsibility of the staff under an executive or administrator. By avoiding direct involvement with operational and administrative matters, the trustees maintain the objectivity necessary for effective supervision.

How can policy be distinguished from administration? Policy always covers the general and is concerned with principles, while administration is the detailed execution of those principles on a daily basis. It may require great restraint in certain circumstances, but a trustee should avoid imposing his personal administrative, esthetic, political or social views upon staff or interfering with prerogatives at the staff level of operation. The general, structural and basic aspects of management are his proper sphere.

A board member will, of course, take an interest in the museum's day-to-day operations, and he may want to confer with the museum director or senior administrative officer on various aspects of institutional management. But he should not instruct the officer to do anything, nor should he criticize any action the executive has taken. If the trustee feels that a problem in management exists, it is his duty to take it to the chairman of the board, the appropriate board committee or the entire board. Directives must be issued only by decision of the board as a collective. If they come from individual trustees, the professional competence of the director is impugned and staff initiative discouraged.

Trustees serving on committees of the board that oversee specific activities of the institution such as fund raising, exhibits or education will have frequent contact with the staff. Under these circumstances it is often difficult to maintain the proper distance from operating detail. The trustee may find it necessary to qualify his statements or ideas as personal opinion only and to make it clear that he is not speaking for the board.

The trustee does become directly concerned with administrative detail when he participates in his board's monitoring and assessment function. Board members are in the best position to assess the institution's progress under the policies they have set, but here they must remain in a review and advisory role, much like that of an accountant who audits an organization's activities after the fact.

Sometimes a trustee becomes involved in executing specific administrative tasks: he may volunteer to assist in a fund-raising project, serve as a docent or perform a particular skill needed by the institution. Changing roles in this manner is difficult but often necessary, especially in small museums that must depend upon assistance from volunteers. If the trustee serves in a voluntary capacity, he will be subject to direction from the appropriate staff supervisor. The trustee who can demonstrate a proper attitude when working for the museum as a volunteer will gain respect from the staff for his role as trustee.

## POLICY STATEMENTS

Once the trustee has understood and accepted his role as policy maker, how does he find sources for the museum's policies? Every organization has a charter, constitution or articles of incorporation that give it legal life and permanence and expound basic principles or fundamental or general purposes. The charter may specify only that the organization's purpose is "to operate a museum for the citizens of ———," but over the years that general statement will have been elaborated in resolutions and actions taken at meetings of the board, which are recorded in its minutes. Traditions will no doubt have accumulated over time concerning the kinds of activities the museum pursues, and these should give at least some direction for future enterprises.

Another source of information about a museum's purposes is the museum's application for tax-exempt status; the Internal Revenue Service demands a cogent explanation of purpose from a nonprofit organization seeking that additional favored classification. The record of gifts or donations of objects the museum has accepted can also reveal much about the goals of the institution. Gifts of cash and other liquid assets frequently contain conditions on use of the money. Moreover, regardless of what the organizational documents might specify, the museum may have developed, over the years, a tradition of accepting certain types of objects.

If no formal statement of purpose exists, the board should consider drafting one. This statement is an up-to-date, concise summary of all the available documents, resolutions and operating traditions of the institution. Committing the museum's purposes and implementing policies to writing does not mean, however, that they cannot be changed. Indeed, policies can and should be susceptible to amendment to retain flexibility of operation. But a written statement of purpose is an important document to have, for it can be submitted to new trustees, funding sources, employees, members of the museum's constituency, prospective donors and any member of the public who is interested in the museum and its operation.

In addition, many museums assemble their charter, constitution, articles of incorporation or other founding documents, and their basic resolutions, bylaws, statement of purpose and all specific policy statements, in a format such as a loose-leaf binder, which can be given to new trustees and others who need current information about the museum. Such a compendium demonstrates that the museum knows what its purposes are and how it intends to achieve its goals.

The board's effort to state purpose and policies as presently understood and practiced may reveal that the museum's purpose has changed significantly from that written in the charter or founding document. If necessary, the charter may be amended. The services of an attorney are needed. If the museum was established as a nonprofit corporation in a simple incorporation, the attorney files amended articles of incorporation after all required notifications and approvals have been accomplished; they frequently include the formal vote of two-thirds of the trustees and two-thirds or more of the members with voting rights. If the museum was founded according to directions in a will or trust document, formal approval of a court is also usually required, as well as the cooperation of the state attorney general.

Amendments can and should be made when necessary, so that the basic documents conform to the museum's actual purposes and the museum is assured of the ability to adapt and survive with the passage of time. Intentional alteration of the course, direction or purpose of an institution, however, should be effected only after the most careful deliberation and full compliance with applicable legal requirements.

By their nature museums are permanent institutions. Without a clear statement of purpose, an institution may dissipate its resources in activities that are only peripheral to its main goals. Because of this tendency, the board should define the goals that are attainable with present and potentially available resources and concentrate on the translation of basic documents into operational policies. Clarifying and implementing the objectives of the museum are therefore part of the trustees' overall responsibility to protect the museum as an entity.

Survival is not the only criterion, however, and there are times when dissolution and transfer of the collections and other assets are the only prudent steps. Because of moral and legal obligations to donors and the general responsibility of museums for maintaining significant objects and specimens, every effort must be made to ensure the preservation and unity of the collections. A diligent search will likely identify an institution willing and able to acquire the collections and assume responsibility for their preservation. Sale of a failing museum's objects on the commercial market is not an acceptable course of action. Total disposition must be a last resort, and for those institutions with permanent collections, sustaining existence and preserving the cultural resources thus committed must be paramount.

# ᓚᓚᓚᓚᓚᓚ Specific Policy Making

Having defined the general purposes of the museum, the board can translate general intent into a series of specific guidelines and policies, from which staff can determine operational plans and procedures. Some areas these policies and guidelines might address are treated in the following pages. The sources listed in Further Readings provide additional information.

## LONG-RANGE PLANNING

The board can help secure its museum's future survival by budgetary planning and sound financial projection. Nonprofit institutions are discovering the value of long-range strategic and financial planning as a means of balancing anticipated resources against future financial needs. The board's insistence upon such planning will demonstrate its commitment to permanence, to systematic growth and to the wise utilization of revenues and funding from outside sources. A detailed five-year plan, or one reaching even further into the future, is an invaluable administrative tool and concrete evidence of committed management. Private donors, foundations and government sources all are impressed by planning drawn up in detail on this level, and the increased funding and assistance a long-range plan stimulates will far exceed the cost of its preparation and updating. The plan should be revised each year on the basis of current activities and funding in the most recent fiscal period.

Conceptualizing and drafting the long-range plan might be done by the museum director and senior staff with assistance from either an *ad hoc* committee of the board or individual trustees. Special training seminars for the drafting team are often beneficial. If additional advice is needed, the team might seek the voluntary assistance of outside specialists, such as educators who can identify the educational needs of the community, scholars who can advise on the optimum research potential of the collections and businessmen who can recommend ways in which the museum might approach the business community. Community leaders familiar with local government, philanthropic institutions and other organizations might offer suggestions for obtaining maximum support for the museum. If voluntary aid is unavailable, the drafting team may decide to hire a consultant experienced in long-range planning.

## ATTENTION TO THE TAX EXEMPTION

Tax-exempt status is fundamental to the nature of a museum; indeed it is part of the definition of a museum for accreditation by the American Association of Museums. It is a classification, however, that does not automatically come with incorporation as a nonprofit corporation. To obtain tax-exempt status, separate application must be made to federal tax authorities. State and local governments will also exempt museums from most if not all real property taxes, although some jurisdictions may demand small payments in lieu of taxes to help pay for essential community services such as fire and police protection. Tax exemption relieves museums of the obligation to pay state and federal income taxes on any net surpluses generated. Museums may also qualify, in addition, for exemption from payment of state and city sales taxes on items purchased for institutional use, although normally museums must collect sales tax on merchandise sold to the public. In addition to these benefits, tax exemption also makes the museum eligible for funds from foundations and government agencies and encourages private donations through the tax deductions available to donors.

The most desirable status for a museum from a donor's point of view is that of a publicly supported charity under the U.S. Internal Revenue Code. For a museum to qualify as a publicly supported charity, as a general rule it must receive at least one-third of its support from a wide circle of private individuals, admission fees or government grants. Charities are certified by the Internal Revenue Service in several categories according to the type and amount of gifts and contributions received from the public, revenues, and the number of donors and supporters. Some special taxes can be assessed against organizations that have minimal gifts or contributions from the public and a small number of donors and supporters. Such charities are called "private foundations" or "private operating foundations."

Trustees should be aware that it is desirable to secure basic financial support for their museum from as many donors and supporters as possible. The regulations in this area are complex, and to preserve the most favorable possible tax status the board will need the advice of a lawyer or an accountant who specializes in tax-exempt organizations.

Museums and other nonprofit organizations are turning more and more to merchandise sales and related commercial activities as sources of operating revenue. As these enterprises could endanger the museum's tax-exempt status, they require special consideration by the board. Should the museum's commercial activities overshadow its educational functions, its tax-exempt status could be revoked. Thus the board needs to establish policies governing all revenue-producing activities, including museum shops, publications and the licensing of reproductions of museum objects. The policies should set controls to protect the museum's tax-exempt status; they might also ensure that the commercial activities reflect a positive image of the museum. In addition, the board should be aware that net surplus on sales of merchandise not related to the purposes of a museum—science books, for example, sold by an art museum—might be subject to taxation as unrelated income. The rates of taxation are similar to those applicable to businesses. Federal and state tax authorities have increased their oversight of the commercial activities of nonprofit organizations.

The board should also be aware that certain types of political or legislative advocacy may endanger the museum's tax-exempt status. For example, a tax-exempt organization may not endorse political candidates or otherwise seek to influence an election. It may, however, appeal to a legislature on a matter directly affecting the institution or at their written request provide law-makers with information upon a matter of public concern. Even some grass-roots lobbying is permissible if small in relation to the museum's total activity. If lobbying will be a relatively large part of the total activity, a special status can be applied for. The trustees' concern in this area is important, and advice of tax counsel should be sought, especially if the museum's programs appear to involve significant marshaling of citizen support for changes in public policies or frequent unsolicited presentations to legislative bodies.

## COMPLIANCE WITH REGULATORY LAWS

Museums have been receiving an increasing amount of their funding from government sources. With this money come re-quirements designed to use the leverage of funding from the public treasury to implement programs such as nondiscrimination and access for the handicapped. Even though the museum may have attempted to avoid discrimination and be accessible to all, the board of an institution receiving government grants should double check that programs, objectives and written policies are in line with current regulations. Written assurance of compliance must be given to obtain government money, and trustees are ultimately responsible for the institution's compliance to government policy and practice.

Aside from the requirements that accompany acceptance of government grants, museums must comply with many other federal and state laws. These specify health and safety conditions in the workplace, safety precautions for visitors and compliance with building and fire codes, and may regulate other aspects of institutional operations.

Another set of laws makes provision for payment of minimum wages to employees and requires that certain personnel be paid for all overtime work. Trustees should be aware of the requirements for payment of employee withholding taxes to state and federal income tax officials, for board members could be personally liable for amounts due government taxing authorities. A museum and its employees may elect to be included in the federal social security system; if the decision is yes, the museum has affirmative duties to contribute to that system.

Some states require that employees be covered by the state's workmen's compensation insurance system. In other jurisdictions coverage is optional for employees of nonprofit organizations. The organization may elect to insure itself against employee claims under the state workmen's compensation system or to arrange for some other kind of protection against employee claims for work-related injuries.

The board has to be thoroughly aware of the extent to which all local, state and federal laws apply to the institution, for it is ultimately responsible for ensuring compliance with these laws and regulations.

## COLLECTIONS MANAGEMENT

Although the museum director is charged with the actual care of the collections, it must be reemphasized that final responsibility for the collections rests with the board. To translate this obligation into detailed, effective guardianship, a collections management policy is required and should be a high priority. This statement specifies what the institution collects and its procedures for accepting gifts. It also defines policies for loaning, conserving, insuring and deaccessioning the objects it owns.

ACQUISITIONS. Museums cannot acquire indiscriminately, and no museum should attempt to collect everything. It is the board's duty to establish a procedure for deciding what objects should be purchased or accepted as donations and to specify levels for approval that may vary with the value of an object or its importance to the collections. Donors frequently attempt to impose express conditions upon acceptance, such as agreement to the permanent display or perpetual holding of the object. As a general rule, objects encumbered with restrictions or conditions should not be accepted. If a donation with conditions attached is nonetheless deemed a desirable acquisition, it should be accepted only with the approval of the full board, for the acceptance carries with it policy-level obligations for care and utilization.

The museum should obtain a clear title to every object it acquires, and the collections management policy might make a clear title imperative. The policy also sets standards for the registration of all objects brought into the museum, whether permanently or on loan, and for accessioning and cataloging. As part of its review function the board should ascertain that all records are complete and up to date.

LOANS. The collections management policy states the conditions under which the museum's objects will be loaned, with levels of approval varying with the object's importance. Certain objects should be loaned only with authorization by the board. Items of lesser importance might be loaned under an approval procedure administered by the museum director.

CONSERVATION. Statements on the care and conservation of the museum's objects are important components of the collections management policy. The board demonstrates its commitment to the objects within its trust with guidelines for their maintenance, security and conservation. The guidelines for accreditation by the American Association of Museums contain basic standards for the care and preservation of objects.

INSURANCE. The board also determines policy on insuring the collections. It decides whether all, or part or none of the collections should be afforded insurance protection, and under what circumstances. In any policy that is purchased, the board should decide upon the deductible. The greater the deductible, the cheaper the insurance premiums, but the more the museum will have to pay before the insurance company will reimburse. A museum's insurance plan for its collections will depend upon finances and other considerations, including probability of losses by fire and theft. Some institutions elect to increase security measures and carry minimum, if any, insurance for the collections when they are on the museum's premises. Better security will, however, decrease the cost of any insurance purchased.

DEACCESSIONING. A crucial part of the collections management policy concerns deaccessioning, or the disposal of objects owned by the museum. This step must be approached with great care. No museum's holdings can remain forever static, and while a museum should rise above current fashion in taste, it should be able to dispose of certain objects, particularly if after appropriate deliberation the museum board decides to concentrate its collecting interests in one area and deemphasize another. Then, too, better examples within a genre may be acquired, and the museum should be able to dispose of the lesser specimens. If an object in the collections was accepted on the condition that it would not be sold, the board is bound by past promises. A complete collections management policy will specify that the records of such an object indicate it is not to be sold. Variance from such a promise can be granted by a court if the museum demonstrates good reason for disposition notwithstanding its original commitment.

Typically the board approves the deaccessioning of an object following recommendation of the director. Some museums set a priority upon placing deaccessioned objects in other institutions and may be willing to receive less than current market values to accomplish that end. This is the preferred policy for items of high cultural or scholarly value, as it ensures that they will remain in the public domain. For objects with limited sale value, such as some natural history specimens or analogous items, the question may be where and whether to transfer or exchange for research purposes. Other museums with marketable collections may be required by law or policy to receive the highest possible price, regardless of where the objects may be placed. The deaccessioning policy, therefore, should make provision for decisions regarding the destination of items being considered for disposal, depending upon their relative cultural, scientific and monetary values. Many museums specify as a matter of policy that proceeds from the sale of deaccessioned objects be used to replenish the collections.

The preferred method of sale should be stated in the collections management policy. Direct sales to private individuals can risk public criticism even with solid appraisals. For example, dealers must increase the price they pay for an object by an amount sufficient to cover their expenses and assure some profit, and too many museums have seen their recently deaccessioned items resold at a substantial markup. Such situations invite unfortunate comment and implications that the institution was careless or even dishonest in its valuation. Because of the volatility in the market for museum-quality collectibles, many institutions specify that deaccessioned objects be sold only at public auction.

The collections management policy ought to specify whether board members and staff are eligible to acquire objects from the collections. Customarily, museum staff and trustees are not allowed to purchase these objects. Some museums forbid the staff, trustees or members of their families to purchase them even at public auction to ensure that no taint of self-interest or inside information clouds the deaccessioning process.

## THE PHYSICAL PLANT

The buildings and grounds are a priority concern of the board. They must provide a secure environment for the collections, protecting them from such threats as fire, theft, vandalism, water and light damage, mildew and pollution. And as standards for the preservation, conservation and exhibition of objects become more strict, the museum's facilities may have to be upgraded. Appropriate temperature and humidity controls, for example, may need to be installed to ensure the proper care of certain kinds of objects.

Not only are museum facilities expensive to construct or renovate, but they require an exceptionally high quality of maintenance as well. The sheer volume of museum attendance puts strains on the physical plant, and the board must ensure that the museum is safe for people as well as for objects.

It is inevitable, then, that the museum's facilities will require the board's constant attention. For this reason a full tour of the museum building—public areas as well as work and storage areas—is an important part of the orientation program for every new trustee, and all members of the board should participate in periodic tours.

## USE OF THE COLLECTIONS
## AND RELATED ACTIVITIES

The trustee's duty to the museum's collections does not end with the assurance they are secure and well housed, managed and conserved. As museum objects are important cultural and educational resources reflecting the history of man and his world, the trustees also have an obligation to see that they are used for scholarly research and for the public's education and spiritual enrichment. Objects ought to be displayed as frequently as their intrinsic ability to withstand reasonable use and the museum's facilities will allow. The board can ensure that the museum fulfills its educational role by setting policies that balance the often competing demands of preservation versus use of the collections. It also needs to establish guidelines for the direction and orientation of exhibitions. An exhibits policy for a children's museum, for example, will require that displays and programs are appropriate to the age levels served by the museum.

Exhibition and loan policies are only part of public access. Guidelines for research should facilitate study of the collections by members of the staff and identify others, from the curious high school student to the renowned scholar, who should be encouraged to use the museum's facilities.

Too often boards lose sight of the uses of the museum and, in their concentration on acquisitions and plant construction, neglect their responsibility to ensure that the museum and its collections involve as broad a segment of the public as feasible. The board first decides if the institution's purposes are best achieved by emphasizing programs addressed to the general public, to scholarly research or to other special ends. It then establishes policies that will allow the museum to use its resources efficiently and serve its constituencies well.

Museums have great potential as focal points for activities that may not grow directly out of the permanent collections or objects on display. These, too, can serve to involve and educate the public. Museums are natural centers for classes on a variety of topics as well as for lecture, film and concert series. In addition, they often sponsor educational tours. The board may want to encourage staff to utilize the institution for appropriate educational programs. Guidelines and procedures can be established to ensure that the capacities of the organization and its physical plant are not overtaxed.

# ⌐⌐⌐⌐ Financial Responsibilities

The very existence of any museum depends upon its financial base, for which trustees have a primary responsibility. They are the keepers of the treasury; they function as overseers for the maintenance, use, augmentation and accounting of their institution's financial resources.

## PLANNING AND BUDGETING

Trustees have an important interest in the museum's annual budget, for the board is responsible for allocation of the museum's resources. The budget is the customary device for applying resources to designated purposes. Attention to the budget is also a primary step in fiscal planning, and much can be learned by comparing budgeted versus actual expenses. Too many museum boards routinely accept the director's proposed budget without any critical examination; such *pro forma* approvals are really an abdication of responsibility.

The director should prepare the budget for the next fiscal year many months in advance and submit it to the board. Annotations can stress particular points that represent changes in direction in expenditures or areas of expected fiscal problems. The board, with the help of the appropriate committees, can then carefully scrutinize the proposed budget, altering it as necessary before approving the fiscal operating plan that will be the basis for the museum's upcoming programs.

The board's function is to authorize and oversee expenditures, but the actual administration of the budget is the province of the staff. This distinction between authorization and administration should be scrupulously observed. The board authorizes existing staff positions by approving budgeted personnel costs, and it should authorize new staff positions as well. The director should be given full authority to fill all staff positions, however, except perhaps for his second-in-command, whose selection and appointment can be made by the director subject to the approval of the board. The board might want this veto power because the second-in-command sometimes serves as acting director.

Any venture with significant financial impact—positive or negative—should be scrutinized by the board and approved in concept before its initiation. New departures from routine operation, such as the establishment of a lecture or performance series, are matters for board consideration, as are plans for major exhibitions. Proposals to charge admission fees, raise membership dues, request donations from visitors or open a museum gift shop also require board approval. In addition, the board should establish guidelines and procedures whereby the director brings ongoing budgetary questions before the board.

## FUND RAISING

The traditional method of fund raising for a museum has been to depend upon gifts from individual donors, especially to pay for major acquisitions and construction of new facilities. This approach is seldom adequate, however, to ensure that the needs of the institution are met. Seeking funds is a major responsibility of board members, but a task many dislike. Yet, if placed in the perspective of an individual's participation in the allocation of society's resources to the most deserving of its educational institutions, fund raising can give the trustee great personal satisfaction. Museums must compete for their share of the charitable dollar to survive, and trustees should take deep pride in helping their institutions achieve their funding goals.

Careful advance planning is necessary to secure a sound financial base for operations and expansion. The museum's goals, priorities and strategies are set by the board. There must be clear statements about how much money will be needed within a defined period, what it will be used for and how the objectives will be achieved.

Every trustee should participate in establishing funding plans and policies, although those who sit on a fund-raising or development committee will be more directly involved with their implementation. The policies established should be broad and imaginative, and all feasible sources explored and included in the plan for potential financing. Special events such as fairs and festivals have funding potential and can create good community public relations.

Programs for deferred giving by individual donors have become a part of institutional fund raising. In these programs the donor transfers property to a bank or other trustee. The organization is the ultimate beneficiary, but the donor continues to receive the income from the property during his lifetime. After his death the institution succeeds to full ownership. The board should approve in concept and organization these programs and all such fund-raising ventures.

Membership groups can yield both short- and long-term financial support. The board should provide for review of these fund-raising activities and for all those undertaken by the museum's affiliate or support groups as well. Because such groups act in the name of the museum and their actions are frequently construed by the public as board activities, their coordination warrants the attention of the board or one of its committees and should not be delegated solely to the museum's development officer.

Museums have been receiving an increasing amount of their funding from government, foundations and corporations, through grants and other means. Some local governments will cooperate with a museum by arranging, usually with voter authorization, for a special bond issue to raise money for the museum. The funds from sale of the bonds can be either a loan to the museum or repaid from the government treasury. Whether a loan or a gift, the museum has the advantage of using the government's powers to borrow money.

Trustees will want to be familiar with the potential for assistance from government and other sources. The interested trustee can learn about the availability of grants from books, articles, seminars and abbreviated courses on this topic. The museum director or staff development officer is usually in charge of the procedural and administrative aspects of institutional fund raising, but the individual trustee might work on an informal basis with the director and staff, making certain that all his efforts are in coordination with theirs. The trustee might suggest receptive sources, write supporting letters or, at appropriate times, make visits to prospects and foundation officials. Foundations, corporations and government granting agencies welcome and need well-reasoned proposals from organizations with sound management backed by knowledgeable and enthusiastic boards.

The museum board should ensure that all appropriate grant funding is obtained. But grants carry a heavy obligation to complete the work proposed, so the board must at the same time be certain that the museum's management, accounting, scheduling and technical resources are adequate to accomplish the promised tasks. The average institution will be awarded between 10 and 20 percent of the grants applied for, but all the awards may come at once. Since a grantor may demand completion of the project within a stated period, careful attention must be paid to scheduling in making grant applications and in accepting grants. Starting or completion dates may sometimes be postponed, but if acceptance of a grant would clearly overtax the museum's capacities, it should be refused. In these circumstances it is far better for the museum to reapply at a later date, and so maintain a reputation for reliability with the granting source, than to default on its commitments.

The board has to ascertain that financial and accounting support and control are adequate so that grant reports are submitted on time and funds used for the expenses authorized. Grants are usually awarded to accomplish specific projects because officials of the grantor institution want particular work done. Depending upon the nature of the grant, it may be unethical or illegal to apply grant money to purposes other than those specified, including use for general operating support. Misapplication of government grants can carry serious legal penalties.

The acceptance of each grant should, therefore, be approved by the board or accepted according to guidelines preestablished by the trustees. Express approval of all grants or a grants policy is necessary because priorities in museum activities frequently must be rearranged to carry out grant proposals.

The board needs to be aware that although grants provide funds, they may also have a negative financial impact on the institution. The museum committed to a project may be compelled to complete it out of its own resources if the original grant funds should prove insufficient. Many grants require the recipient institution to contribute or match part of the costs, and even though the matching funds may be supplied by another granting source, the grant itself must often be accepted before this supplementary funding is secured. If it does not materialize, the museum may need to use its reserves to carry out the project.

## INVESTMENT AND CASH MANAGEMENT

Close supervision of the management of institutional endowments is a traditional task of trustees, frequently assigned as the special responsibility of one or more finance or investment committees. It is the duty of trustees to manage all the financial assets of their trust so that maximum gain is realized within the bounds of what is considered prudent investment. Trustees are responsible for ensuring that all the museum's financial resources, including the cash needed for day-to-day operations, are put to the most efficient and profitable use. Balances in non-interest-bearing bank accounts ought not to exceed the minimum levels needed for immediate cash requirements.

Supervision of restricted or endowment funds is frequently assigned to the finance committee. Every board member, however, should be familiar with the terms and restrictions on major bequests and endowment gifts, for the entire board is legally responsible for compliance with all binding conditions. Legal counsel can be secured if questions arise regarding the power to use the principal of an endowment fund or to apply income from a restricted endowment to a purpose not specified in the governing instrument, or if there are doubts that a gift designated for a particular purpose is being used correctly. It is possible to petition a court for judicial blessing of a change of direction in use of a fund, but in most states the attorney general's office should be consulted first and often made a party to the action before the court.

The board will be wise to insist that separate accounts are kept for each restricted or endowment fund, and the museum's auditors may require them. Without separate accounts, funds may be improperly utilized, or, at the very least, confusion will arise as to whether a fund is being spent only for authorized purposes. Some funds carry with them special restrictions and can only be used for specific, well-defined purposes. These are often referred to as "designated funds." An institution should be able to demonstrate plainly the additions to and expenditures from all funds.

Institutions with an appreciable amount of funds may retain an outside investment manager. Contracting with an investment management firm is a board decision made upon recommendation of the finance committee, often with the advice of the museum director. Special care must be exercised to ensure that this decision is objective. Many authorities recommend that the firm selected have no ties or obligations to any member of the board or museum staff or to their families. It sometimes happens, however, that a banker or investment manager sitting on the board is a member of the firm that manages the museum's accounts. As such a situation inevitably invites allegations of conflict of interest, it must be entered into only with full disclosure and documentation of the circumstances, including a statement of why this contract is clearly advantageous to the museum. This documentation should be included as part of the board's official proceedings. The board generally evaluates the performance of investment managers at least once a year, and should retain the option to change firms.

## ACCOUNTING AND AUDIT

Competent accounting of the museum's income and expenses is essential if the board members are to perform effectively their role as financial overseers. The smaller museum may find that daily bookkeeping by a staff member who has some business training is sufficient, but larger institutions generally employ a bookkeeper or someone trained in accounting. The staff bookkeeper's work should be checked at intervals by an accountant, and all bookkeeping and accounting should be supplemented with an annual audit by an independent accounting firm that will prepare year-end statements. The auditor is selected by the board, and, to assure the independence of the audit, the firm must not have any ties or obligations to board members. Some accounting authorities recommend a change of audit firms every four or five years to assure a fresh look at the museum's financial operation, although it may be sufficient for different personnel of the same firm to take on the assignment. The audit should be prepared for and submitted to the board. It is the trustees who bear ultimate responsibility for the museum's assets, and they will be held accountable for lapses in financial management as nonprofit organizations are subjected to tougher standards in the years to come.

By providing for audited financial statements, the board demonstrates that it understands its fiscal responsibilities. In the course of preparing the museum's financial reports the auditors will examine the institution's financial management and recommend to the board any action necessary to tighten fiscal controls. Outside professional advice is an invaluable aid in helping the board oversee the flow and maintenance of institutional assets.

The financial reports—typically a balance sheet and a statement of income and expenses for the period under review—should be clear and include a statement that they were prepared in accordance with generally accepted accounting principles. Donors and grantors, both governmental and private, increasingly look at audited financial statments as a measure of their prospective recipient's fiscal control and financial health, and some major donors and grantors require them. A museum's financial reports should also be available to the public to demonstrate that the trustees acknowledge their institution's accountability for the public assets under their control. Financial reports presented in an intelligible format suggest to the lay reader the museum's competence in the utilization of its resources and the permanence of its operation. In most membership organizations the members have a right to be presented with annual financial reports.

Some organizations require the director or the accountant to prepare monthly financial statements to keep a continual check on patterns of cash flow, income and expenses. Such interim financial reports might be prepared quarterly. In any event, it is a fundamental obligation of the director to keep the board fully informed of the financial health of the museum, and this must be done on a current basis. Without some type of frequently prepared financial reports, the director will not be able to meet that responsibility. For their part, the board members have a duty to keep themselves well acquainted with the current financial status of the institution.

## FINANCIAL SUPPORT
## FOR THE GOVERNMENT MUSEUM

Many museums supported by a city, county or state governmental unit draw a major percentage of their funding as annual subsidies or appropriations from the public treasury. Other types of government support include civil service personnel detailed to work for the museum and buildings or other property made available to the museum. Taxpayers in some localities have voted maximum limits on property tax assessments or otherwise curtailed the spending powers of their local governments, and museums in these areas must compete with their community's vital services—fire, police and road departments—for the limited funds, civil service personnel and property that remain. In such cases the museum board must exert great effort to ensure that its institution is an essential community resource and perceived as such by those who dispense government support to local cultural organizations. Sometimes deep cuts in government support cannot be forestalled even when the board has demonstrated its commitment to the public good by effective management of the museum's resources. Then other funding resources must be developed, such as corporations, membership drives, admission charges or donations, and expansion of sales in the museum's shop.

# ᄅᄅᄅᄅᄅ The Board and the Staff

Despite its primary role as policy maker and overseer, the board carries some responsibilities for administration of the museum and its staff. It functions as the final authority for the actual execution of its policies as translated into practice by the museum director and the staff.

## THE DIRECTOR

The board's foremost administrative task is the selection and supervision of the chief executive, referred to in most museums as the director. He has the responsibility for operational management and appoints and directs the staff.

Board members will likely find it difficult to oversee the director's performance without interfering with his prerogatives in the sphere of his duty, but this fine distinction must be observed with dignity on both sides. The director must be allowed enough independence to exercise his initiative and yet be assured of the board's support of his performance and objectives. This balance of responsibility between board and director will be facilitated by a carefully drafted job description that delineates the director's sphere of action and his duties.

## PERSONNEL POLICIES

A responsibility of the board toward staff, although not directly supervisory, is the establishment of sound personnel policies and procedures. A major portion of the museum's budget will be staff salaries, training and benefits, so board attention to a personnel policy is warranted from a purely fiscal standpoint. Policies ought to provide for staff training and opportunities for professional advancement. Staff should be considered to include volunteers, for though unpaid, their training, coordination and supervision involve a museum expenditure. The paid and volunteer staff can be the museum's most valuable resource if its members are able to function in a framework of personnel policies that provide predictability and a sense that the institution esteems their individual contributions. There is an emerging concept of professionalism among museum staff, which extends to volunteers as well. The board should make sure that the institution is attuned to the demand for increased staff responsibility, autonomy and employee rights.

LEGAL RIGHTS.   The traditional view of the employer-employee relationship allows the employer all the prerogatives and the right to control or discharge the employee at will. Collective bargaining rights, union contracts and rights under law have altered the balance for some employees. Civil rights laws have added another dimension to personnel rights, restricting employers from discriminatory employment practices on the basis of race, color, religion, sex, age or handicapped status.

Beyond the civil rights laws is expanded recognition of some fundamental constitutional rights in the employment context. As of 1981, only those employees who work in government and government-affiliated organizations have been allowed to assert rights to free speech and due process of law in challenging discipline or dismissal. Institutions that are not closely integrated with a governmental unit, such as a city, county or state, so far are not held to be subject to the free speech and due process mandates of the U.S. Constitution. The free speech cases typically have involved written or oral statements by employees that provoked their governmental unit employer to take action against them. The due process cases have focused on arbitrary actions by the governmental employer. Boards responsible for museums that are government supported should be aware of the legal situation of their institutions vis-à-vis employees' constitutional rights, and all other museum boards should watch legal developments with regard to their staffs' abilities to claim federal or state constitutional protection. Constitutional rights are a complex area of law that cannot be ignored. Museum officers and trustees can be held personally liable for infringements, hence the need for experienced legal counsel when such questions arise.

In addition to standard provisions regarding time off and fringe benefits, personnel policies should speak to all facets of employees' legal rights. The policies must face the legal complexities of all civil rights laws applicable to the institution as employer and ensure that the constitutional rights of employees are accorded full recognition. Personnel policies should also make reference to the health and safety rights of employees, for under various laws employees are guaranteed certain rights to complain, without fear of retaliation, of conditions in the workplace that they believe to be unsafe. The boards of those museums that have collective bargaining agreements with segments of the work force should approve draft personnel policies only after it is determined that they are consistent with terms agreed to in the contracts with employee unions.

GRIEVANCE PROCEDURES. An important part of personnel policies and procedures is the grievance machinery, usually provided as a courtesy to employees and to save administrative time and expense, although sometimes also required by the terms of union contracts. Boards should ensure that procedures are established for dealing with personnel complaints and that every avenue for settling complaints within the institution is made available. Litigation can be prohibitively expensive, and if an employee files suit the museum may be compelled to settle out of court rather than commit its cash reserves to a costly legal battle. An intelligently thought out grievance procedure can provide for the resolution of most employee complaints before a great deal of time or money is required for legal defense.

The grievance procedure generally involves the board directly, but only as a body of last resort within the museum. Most grievances will be decided by the museum director or one of his chief assistants, but employees should be able to appeal to the board or one of its committees if they are not satisfied with determinations made at the museum administrative level. Typically an employee appeal is heard by the personnel committee or an *ad hoc* committee of the board. The committee reports its recommendation to the full board, which approves or modifies the decision, making it a board determination. Depending upon his style and philosophy of management, the director may consider an employee's appeal to the board as a sign of fundamental incompatibility between himself and that individual. From the museum's perspective, however, an appeal to the board is preferable to a lawsuit. Therefore the board may attempt to counsel the director to take the view that such appeals do not reflect negatively on his management but can represent honest differences of opinion.

When hearing employee appeals, the board should have experienced legal counsel to advise during every part of the procedure. If a grievance is carried as far as the board, most employees will have retained counsel, and the board should have an equally sophisticated legal adviser. A poorly handled appeal at this level can lay the basis for legal action against the museum and the board, including possible liability on the part of board members who participated in the appeal decision. Counsel can steer these trustees through current legal precedent and ensure that the employee's rights are not violated. If the question is to be resolved inside the organization, the board's decision must be final.

# ⌐ Assessing Museum Operations

The board is ultimately responsible for all aspects of the museum's operations, and so it has the additional task of assessing those operations to determine how well policies are succeeding in practice. As guardians of the organization's preferred tax-exempt status and its reputation in the local community in particular and the museum world in general, the trustees are in a good position to assess the growth or possible decline of the museum's goodwill and to determine whether its basic character as a nonprofit, educational organization has been enhanced or eroded by activities as either planned or practiced.

All activities of the museum, from its exhibitions, education and outreach programs and collections management to its museum shops, should be reviewed to ascertain their success in meeting departmental and individual program goals and the relation of achievements to the museum's larger purposes. Review should also include administrative operations generally and, specifically, personnel policies, fiscal and grants administration and aspects of operations such as accessibility for the handicapped. Particular attention should be given to the equal opportunity and nondiscrimination aspects of personnel matters, which contain a great potential for conflict between museum management and staff. Review of grants administration is important not only to ensure that all commitments are being met but to assess the impact of the institution's grants management process as it is perceived by the major grantors. Funding agencies sponsoring exhibitions sometimes require an objective assessment of the exhibition's educational effectiveness.

Part of the board's responsibility for policy is to designate those programs and activities that require board approval before they are initiated. Each board should provide its institution's director with guidelines that make clear what matters he is to bring before the board. The guidelines should designate those programs and activities that require board approval before they are initiated and the level of change in existing programs that necessitates the board's attention. One guideline, for example, might specify a percentage of budget overrun for an individual program or department that, if exceeded, would require the director to inform the board. The director must be allowed to exercise his initiative, however, and not feel that he must report on every operating problem and budgetary detail. For questions outside the purview of the guidelines, board responsibility might in practice be confined to discussions between the director and the appropriate committee or committee chairman; the matter could later be reported to the full board.

The board should consider establishing a routine schedule for reviews. With routine scheduling, the director and his division and program chiefs can anticipate and plan for the board's evaluation and should not feel defensive, as they might if a review is called on an *ad hoc* basis.

# ꙰꙰꙰꙰꙰꙰꙰꙰ *Self-Management*

Finally, the board has the responsibility to be effective in its own organization and operation. If it shirks self-management, leaving the museum director to establish its operational framework, schedule its meetings and determine its agenda, the board abdicates its leadership role. It will then either be dominated by the director or degenerate into factionalism; it will seldom act as a collective. A board that does not take responsibility for self-management is often easily manipulated by inside or outside influences—persons eager to promote their own particular interests and activities.

Every board, then, should evaluate its own performance just as it appraises the operations of the museum. While this evaluation can be informal and occasional, much can be learned from some form of self-assessment at specified intervals of one or two years. Members can increase their sense of cohesiveness as a functioning body and learn to work together harmoniously by meeting, for example, at a distant, pleasant location for two days. This kind of extended assembly provides an opportunity for trustees to relax and reflect together and to focus on the problems of governing the board and the museum in a way not possible during a two-hour meeting squeezed in among other daily preoccupations. Such a reflective seminar must be well planned in advance to ensure that the trustees' time and the museum's funds are effectively used.

Specific guidelines for the board in determining its structure and managing its operation are presented in the following chapter.

# III  *Structure and Operation of the Board*

The needs and functions of every museum differ, but there are certain basic considerations common to the establishment or reorganization of every institution's governing board. This chapter suggests guidelines that the board may consider and adapt as will best suit the needs of its institution.

## Size

There is no universal prescription for determining the ideal size of the museum board. In practice, the extent and complexity of institutional operation and the number of qualified persons available for membership will usually be the deciding factors. A primary rule of thumb, however, is that the board should be large enough to fulfill its responsibilities and small enough to act as a deliberative body. Most boards prefer to retain some flexibility as to numbers so that an especially well qualified individual can join when he is available and is not lost to another organization while the museum board waits for a vacancy.

Some museums do well with a board of no more than 10 or 12 members, and the trustees are able to function efficiently in part because of their small numbers. But members of a small board must be prepared to serve on several committees simultaneously or individually to accept responsibility for overseeing more than one area of the museum's operations. As an alternative, the smaller board might appoint outside persons to serve on committees. The bylaws of most nonprofit organizations permit committee service by nontrustees.

A board of 15 to 25 members allows for greater representation and utilization of the skills and experience in the community. A membership exceeding 25 could be appropriate for larger institutions. One obvious disadvantage of the oversized board is the problem of coordinating each individual member's participation; such a board may find it difficult to function as a collective. Moreover, since a large board is often laborious to convene and inefficient in transacting business, it must rely heavily upon the executive committee. Pressure to increase the size of a board can be relieved by establishing a prestigious support group that can grow as needed.

# ᴚᴚᴚᴚ Composition of the Board and Selection of Trustees

Museum trustees are generally elected to board service by vote of the board itself, often upon presentation of a slate of candidates by a nominating committee composed of board members. Suggestions for potential candidates may come from individual trustees as well as from the museum director, for he is in frequent  contact with persons who are interested in the museum. The board should have the opportunity to discuss all potential nominees, and no commitments should be agreed to in the exploratory stage. Indeed, it may be best if the prospective candidate is not aware at this early stage that the board is interested in his nomination. The nominating process can be much more flexible if the list of potential nominees remains confidential to the board. If discretion is exercised, the candidate can be rejected in the preliminary stages without embarrassment to him or to the board. No direct statement that could be construed by the candidate as an offer to join the board should be made by the nominating committee or any individual board member without a vote by the full board.

Museums that are membership organizations elect trustees by vote of the members. The nominating process is conducted by a nominating committee that may include some trustees but acts independently of the board and is the final authority for nomination to board membership. In all organizations, the principle should remain constant that no individual is asked to stand for election until the proper authority has passed upon his candidacy.

A trustee's service to the museum can be utilized in many different ways, and the board should have a clear idea of what perspectives, talents, interests and affiliations would be useful additions to its membership. Some factors to be considered in determining the composition of the board are age and sex distribution. A wide spread in the age of board members is desirable for several practical reasons. Older members contribute experience and wisdom; those in the middle group, because of their active position in the community, carry the major task of relating the museum to its constituency; the younger members, with ability and drive, will receive preparation for greater responsibility in the future. But the primary criteria for trusteeship should be an individual's sense of social responsibility and his desire and ability to render service to the museum. Energy, enthusiasm and dedication to that condition of unselfish service required of a trustee are the important qualities to look for.

The candidate's ability to give substantial time and commitment is also a primary consideration, although some persons may be desirable additions to the board because their talents and affiliations can be used to the museum's great advantage despite the relatively small amount of time they can give. No person should be asked to serve solely because of his affiliations, however. If an individual cannot make the minimum commitment of time required to meet his legal obligations as a trustee and yet has a deep interest in the museum, he might be elected as an outside member of a committee of the board or become a member of an organization supporting or advisory to the institution.

For the board to function efficiently as a working unit, individual trustees must be willing to suppress their differences of temperament and opinion in the broader interests of effective management. The board should consider the general tenor of group interaction whenever possible in the recruiting of new trustees. Too much participation from a single individual can create problems. At the very least, it may discourage the active involvement of other members, who may feel that their contributions are insignificant by comparison. Those whose interest in the museum is restricted to a few areas and does not seem likely to expand will not serve the institution well either. Trusteeship carries with it an obligation to work for the entire museum. A large institution with diverse programs and activities and a board of commensurate size might be able to absorb a few trustees with limited interests, but too many partisans will split the board into factions for each department. To function well the board must objectively provide for all activities and ensure they are coordinated for accomplishing the museum's overall goals. The improved functioning of the board as a body should always be a primary objective in considering candidates for membership.

Boards often seek individuals with special knowledge or skills that relate to the institution's purposes, but these special skills can sometimes cause problems. For example, a trustee who promises to donate incidental professional services as part of his board duty may later attempt to contract with the museum when there is a substantial amount of work to be done in his field. Conflict of interest questions are inherent in contracts with board members for their professional or commercial services, though such arrangements can be advantageous to the museum if properly entered into and documented. In certain areas of low population density, the best-qualified professional available for a particular assignment may be a trustee. The legal ramifications of such situations are discussed in chapter V.

It is traditional for individuals with personal collecting interests similar to those of the museum to be appointed to the board. The person is elected partly because of his expertise, and sometimes with the expectation that he will make occasional donations or perhaps bequeath his collection to the museum. Few questions were raised about these relationships in past years, chiefly because such a trustee was often a major benefactor truly devoted to the museum and in many cases he collected museum-quality pieces for their esthetic rather than their monetary value. But the recent extreme escalation in the price of objects of museum quality has forced many esthetically inclined private collectors to reevaluate their activity in terms of economics. The income tax reduction advantages of gifts to museums can be substantial, and institutions must be aware that a collector may take board membership in order to influence the institution to accept his donations. Actual and apparent conflicts of interest arise if trustee-collectors are placed in positions in which they might exert pressure regarding the acquisition of objects from their personal collections. The same conflicts of interest can also arise regarding the acceptance of loans from a trustee's collection for either exhibition or study. Exhibition of certain objects by a museum can increase their value substantially, and the collector can also benefit merely by having the museum accept custody of an object, as it will then receive institutional security and care. Museum boards should be aware of all these potential problems in considering collectors for board service.

Individuals who have the most to contribute as trustees are also likely to have many existing commitments to personal business affairs and to other organizations. Among a trustee's possible conflicts of interest are associations with business enterprises that could develop commercial relationships with the museum or obligations to other nonprofit organizations that might compete for funding. As a matter of policy, some museum boards will not consider as candidates for membership individuals who are trustees of certain other nonprofit institutions, particularly those that compete with the museum for funding from the same sources. Certain types of personal commitments or professional activities invariably create conflicts of interest with board service. An art dealer, for example, who serves on the board of an art museum may possess valuable expertise, but there is no way that his commercial ties can be set aside, and his very presence on the board calls into question the nonprofit purpose of the museum. The involvement of dealers with the governance of museums should be limited to service on advisory committees, and in some instances even that connection may not be wise.

A broad view ought to be taken regarding conflict of interest questions, with the board alert to all kinds of perceived as well as actual conflicts. If persons outside the museum have a strong impression that there is a conflict of interest, the board may have to issue an explanation even if no actual conflict exists. Because the circumstances of apparent, or perceived, conflict of interest may be complicated and technical, a convincing explanation could be difficult to produce and the credibility of the institution will thus be impaired in the eyes of the public. The board must therefore be prepared to strike from the list of potential nominees a candidate whose services as a trustee cannot be isolated from his outside commitments in a way that preserves the working integrity of the museum and its reputation.

Recognition of conflict of interest is expected from all trustees who serve public purpose institutions. The question of conflict of interest is most easily broached before candidates for board service are formally nominated. The board can direct the nominating committee to introduce frank discussion of possible conflicts during a preliminary interview, at which time it can be determined whether the candidate will have an overlap of personal or organizational commitments that might lead to conflicts of interest if he is elected. All who participate in the preliminary interview should understand that conflicts of interest are inherent to activity in the modern world. If they can be managed while the individual serves as a trustee, they need not be immediately disqualifying. The individual may, for example, be placed only on committees unrelated to his other obligations or be instructed to abstain from discussion or voting on certain issues.

The preliminary interview will also serve to introduce candidates to the duties and responsibilities incumbent upon election to the board. When it is concluded, the nominating committee should have enough information to make a final recommendation of candidates. Those few candidates who appear reluctant to assume the ethical and practical burdens of service are best stricken from the list at this point. Most candidates, however, will welcome the service obligations of museum trusteeship and the opportunity to promote the institution.

To involve certain individuals with the museum in some formal manner, boards are sometimes tempted to elect them as trustees with the tacit understanding that no real participation is expected. But the law does not recognize such a status; if a person has been elected to board membership he is legally responsible for the operation of the organization and to work for its betterment. "Trustee emeritus" or "life trustee" may be appropriate honorifics for members who have completed their service if the bylaws make it clear that such individuals have no further legal obligation. "Honorary trustee" or "advisory trustee" are also possible designations if the bylaws provide that the title does not carry with it the responsibilities of trusteeship or the right to vote on the board. In lieu of such designations, individuals might be elected to membership in support or advisory groups.

The *ex officio* trustee is a board member because he holds some official position, and it is part of the duties of that position to sit as a trustee. *Ex officio* literally means "by virtue of office." Typically, the *ex officio* trustee holds a government position that requires he serve as a trustee of a museum which is part of or substantially supported by that unit of government. As a general rule the *ex officio* board member has the same range of fiduciary responsibilities and liabilities as his fellow trustees.

The objective for every organization should be a dedicated board that is well acquainted with the museum, knowledgeable and realistic about the powers, responsibilities and liabilities of trusteeship and has among its component members the ability to meet the challenges faced by that institution. The needs of particular museums cannot be addressed here, but special requirements may be met by utilizing variations of the suggested search, selection and orientation procedures.

# ꙮꙮꙮꙮꙮ *Orientation for New Board Members*

The board should establish orientation and education programs for its members. Each prospective nominee should be briefed in a preliminary interview on the service obligations of trusteeship and the special responsibilities for trustees of that museum's board. Immediately upon joining the board the new trustee should be further instructed on the extent of his responsibilities. In addition, he will need to study the museum's charter or constitution, basic resolutions and policies and the minutes of the board meetings. These documents will be easily available if assembled in a folder or loose-leaf binder. Additional publications and materials about trusteeship and museums can be a special section of the museum's library. These resources should be studied by both new and experienced trustees, for the more a trustee learns about his role and that of museums, the more successful and rewarding will be his service to his museum and to himself.

The new trustee's study can be augmented by discussion with experienced trustees and by tours of the museum. These will help him see how trusteeship principles are translated into board policies and practices and museum activities. Board members need to know their institution's physical facilities at first hand, and new trustees should arrange with the museum director for a tour of the physical plant. The trustee of a small museum can review the public areas and storage facilities in a short time. The board member of a large institution will have to be more selective in what he sees, but the effort will give him a realistic picture of the museum's needs.

Seeing and experiencing the staff members' work environment will also permit the trustee a better understanding of their problems. In addition, these visits will allow staff members to become informally acquainted with the trustees, who otherwise might exist to them only as an abstraction called "the board." Many staff members have no opportunity to talk with trustees aside from brief formal introductions at museum social functions. While on tour the trustee should avoid discussion of questions more appropriate to the board room or concerning administrative detail. He should make it clear that he is there to observe and learn.

# ᒥᒧᒥᒧᒥᒧᒥᒧ Bylaws and Records

The charter, articles of incorporation or constitution, statement of purpose and appropriate policies formulated by the board guide the substantive and administrative activities of the museum. The articles of incorporation or constitution of a membership organization fixes the rights and responsibilities of the members, who elect the board of trustess. Rules for the board's operation are embedded in the bylaws and related resolutions of the board. Many boards rely upon bylaws from a form book or another organization, but these do not provide for specific situations. Instead, bylaws should be tailored to each board's unique needs. Bylaws must be in accordance with state law, and in drafting them the board should consult legal counsel. Furthermore, bylaws should be kept up to date with amendments that take into account the board's changing organizational requirements and record the resolution of structural and procedural problems. If well drafted and current, they will provide a blueprint for deliberation and action upon important matters of organizational policy for which the board holds ultimate responsibility. They will also be available for individual trustees to consult, and, as a result, board meetings will proceed with greater efficiency.

Bylaws are a protection for the board and its individual trustees. When the specified procedures are followed and there is a record of formal action, board performance cannot be attacked as defective in form. Faithful observance of the bylaws and the scrupulous keeping of minutes and resolutions document that the board acted properly as a body; this documentation protects individual members from allegations that they acted independently of the collective. Even with allegations of conflict of interest or self-dealing, the individual trustee is usually protected from further criticism or liability if the conflicting circumstances were previously disclosed in accordance with the disclosure sections of the bylaws and the minutes reflect that the board acknowledged the disclosure and deemed the corrective measures taken to be sufficient.

## CALLS TO MEETINGS AND ATTENDANCE

Bylaws should set the rules for scheduling meetings and establish the form and length of notice that must be given members before a meeting can be convened. They should specify that an agenda be included with the formal notice of meeting, provide for distribution of committee reports in advance of meetings and lay down a procedure for board action on items not included on the agenda. The bylaws should also provide for emergency meetings. When these are called, each trustee should sign a statement certifying that he was notified of the meeting and waives the regular notice period specified in the bylaws. In either case, quorum rules are important to prevent a minority of members from attempting to act as the full board. Very important acts, such as the adoption of a statement of purpose, should require more than a simple majority of the trustees present and voting.

The bylaws should set standards for trustees' attendance at meetings and diligence in the performance of assigned tasks. They might require that the chairman or another official make inquiry when a trustee misses a specified number of board meetings without explanation. Other commitments or illness may be the reasons, but, even so, the trustee remains accountable for board actions despite his absence. Fairness to him demands that he be removed from continuing responsibility if he cannot take part in those actions for which he could be liable. The absent trustee concerned about a particular course of action might want to send a letter to the board chairman indicating his dissent. Some bylaws include a provision for the recording of postmeeting dissents.

## MINUTES AND RECORDS

Recording consideration of and action on board business is critical, and the bylaws should specify that minutes be kept of all board actions and important committee decisions. Typical board action is by unanimous agreement of those present, but if there are abstentions, dissents or split decisions, the votes of individual trustees should also be recorded. A trustee can usually protect himself from personal liability by recording a dissenting vote to an action of the board he feels particularly unwise. The bylaws should provide for such a procedure, facilitating the individual trustee's dissent and ensuring that his dissenting vote is made a matter of permanent record. Minutes are not generally taken during executive sessions, but a summary of the decisions reached and actions taken should be recorded.

The minutes, as the permanent record, should be kept secure, for they are the principal evidence of the board's functioning over the years. If the bylaws give the board its present life and projected future, the minutes and resolutions are its historical presence, demonstrating that the board met its obligations in a businesslike manner. The elected secretary is usually entrusted with custody of the current book of minutes and resolutions, and prior volumes are kept in a secure archives. All board members should have ready access to the minutes and resolutions, for they are responsible and accountable for all actions taken by the board or in its name. It is a good idea for a duplicate set of minutes and other basic documents, such as the articles of incorporation, charter, constitution and significant board resolutions, to be deposited off the museum's premises in a vault or secure repository.

To make the required record, a recording secretary is present at all meetings except executive sessions. This person might be a reliable employee of the museum assigned as administrative support to the board or an outside person engaged by the board for this purpose. The business of most museum boards involves too much detail to expect the trustee elected as board secretary to record the sessions, though he should oversee the prompt preparation of the minutes and resolutions from the recording secretary's notes. The recording secretary is responsible for sending every board member a copy of the minutes as soon after the meeting as possible. Many boards specify in their bylaws that minutes are to be distributed no later than 30 days after the meeting.

## EXECUTIVE SESSIONS

Executive sessions can be provided for in the bylaws as a regular feature of every board meeting so that appropriate questions can be discussed frankly among museum management officials. In some states museums subject to open-meeting, or "sunshine," laws are prohibited from closing executive sessions to visitors or the public unless there are exceptional circumstances as defined in the law. Open-meeting laws apply, however, only to boards of museums that are government affiliated.

## DISCLOSURE

Bylaws should include provision for disclosure by current board members and prospective trustees of possible conflicts of interest. There should be machinery for submission of updated statements and for the review of all information submitted. Remedies can be specified, such as disqualifying a trustee with a possible conflict of interest from discussing or voting on a particular matter.

## INDEMNIFICATION

As a protective measure for board members, the bylaws should include a provision authorizing the board to indemnify trustees for expenses incurred in defending themselves from charges and lawsuits in connection with board service. This bylaw must be carefully drafted with the assistance of an attorney knowledgeable about applicable state law, so it allows the museum to assist, defend or indemnify its trustees to the maximum extent. Indemnification and insurance protection for trustees are considered further in chapter V.

## ELECTION PROCEDURES

The bylaws should set up nominating and election procedures. In the membership organization, however, it is often the constitution or articles of incorporation that outline how the membership is to select the trustees. Terms of board service should be specified, perhaps three to five years, and be staggered to expire at intervals. This rotation allows for continuity, as there will always be several veterans who can introduce the new appointees to their duties. Limiting the number of terms a trustee can serve prevents individuals with a tendency to dominate from attaining control of the board and ensures periodic infusion of new talent. But there are also disadvantages to limiting terms of appointment, as it sometimes means losing a trustee whose continued participation would be a valuable asset to the board. If there is a limit on consecutive terms, a person whose services the museum wishes to retain can be asked to serve on a committee upon the expiration of his term and at the end of a suitable interval he can be nominated for reelection to the board.

## SELECTION OF CHAIRMAN AND OTHER OFFICERS

The bylaws should provide for selection of the chairman of the board and delineate his authority vis-à-vis the board and the museum's administration. In membership organizations the elected president usually serves as chairman of the board. The chairmanship is the key position in the life of the board and in the success of the institution, and the basis for effective chairmanship is established by the bylaws. The chairman should have the power to coordinate the work of board committees, to call and preside at meetings and, in the absence of an executive committee, to provide guidance between board meetings subject to the approval of the full board.

The bylaws should provide for the selection of other board officers, such as one or more vice-chairmen, the treasurer (who may also be chairman of the finance committee), the board secretary and any additional positions that fit the needs of the particular institution. Typically all officers are elected by the board for terms of not more than two years; they may or may not be eligible to serve successive terms. Officers of membership organizations are usually chosen by vote of the members.

## COMMITTEE STRUCTURE AND SERVICE

The board's basic committee structure should be spelled out in bylaws, where the various standing committees are listed and their purpose and authority stated. Provisions for *ad hoc* committees should include guidelines for their mode of appointment and method of dissolution. As a general principle, an *ad hoc* committee should cease to exist as soon as it completes its work and administrative details, such as the preparation of reports and assembly of whatever records seem appropriate for inclusion in the board's archives. Appointment of advisory committees should be authorized and provided for in the bylaws. Although the chairman or the executive committee might have authority to set up other committees, the full board should act in creating advisory committees since their establishment is a major action and ought to be undertaken only if they have a real function. Many advisory committees seldom if ever meet, and the advisers are used only as endorsements for the organization. Nontrustees should be able to serve on any committee of the board, except the nominating and executive committees, and to vote on committee business. In most museums the nominating and executive committees include only full members of the board, but the membership organization's nominating committee frequently has a majority of nontrustees. Since selection of trustees is a prerogative of the members, they also control the nominating process.

Finally, the bylaws should delineate the relationships between the chairman of the board and committee chairmen, spelling out whether the board chairman has authority to appoint individuals to committees or to name committee chairmen. Those who serve on the nominating, executive and other major committees ought to be elected by the full board. Committees should report to the full board directly, not through the board chairman, and committee reports, including those of the executive committee, should be sent to all trustees in advance of the meeting at which action is to be taken. Many boards have a bylaw that establishes mandatory rotation of chairmanships and appointments to standing committees.

## AMENDING THE BYLAWS

Amending the bylaws should be a simple procedure, requiring only a majority vote of the trustees on the recommendation of the chairman or the committee charged with keeping the bylaws current. For the membership organization, changes in bylaws are to be distinguished from amendment of its basic articles, charter or constitution, which usually requires a vote of at least two-thirds of the membership and sometimes a mail ballot to ensure the rights of all members to participate in the decision.

Bylaws will need to be updated to reflect the changes in operation and distribution of authority within the board. Trustees should receive advance notice of proposed changes; bylaws ought not to be amended during the course of a meeting except to confront true emergency situations. Even then they must be revised in an orderly way and with forethought. It is crucial that all members be supplied with the current version of the bylaws; problems can result if some of the trustees are unacquainted with revisions.

# ㄹㄹㄹㄹㄹㄹㄹ *Committee Structure*

Committees are essential to the conduct of the business of most boards. Each board should determine what committee structure is appropriate to its individual operation. An inappropriate or cumbersome arrangement of committees, with overlapping jurisdiction, can make for an ineffective board and create frustration.

The basic authority and scope of action of each standing committee is generally prescribed in the bylaws, but many boards find it wise to provide a specific charter or written charge for every committee. These documents can be revised frequently in order to prevent overlap or confusion about responsibilities for overseeing a particular concern. The charters for all but standing committees should specify a finite life; committees should not linger on after their mission is accomplished. It is far better to set up a committee of short duration, with the option to extend its life if necessary to complete its tasks, than to allow a committee without an actual mission to go on indefinitely.

Committee functions should not be left only to experts, for that is contrary to the basic concept of lay control of boards. Individuals with expertise and interest in certain areas are often appointed to appropriate committees, but each committee needs some nonspecialists. They provide a link between the other board members and the specialists, keeping the experts aware of the need for committee reports unencumbered by jargon.

Procedures should be established—preferably fixed in the bylaws—to ensure that committee actions and recommendations receive ample review and deliberation by the board before it must vote to approve. Committee reports on all matters should be distributed to all trustees well in advance of the meeting at which actions based upon the reports will be taken. Actions taken by the executive committee, in particular, should be summarized and sent to the trustees before the meeting at which they are asked to ratify its interim decisions. Each trustee is responsible for the board's actions on committee submissions; thus he will have to read committee reports and fully understand the questions referred from committee before casting his vote. If a trustee disagrees with a board action he should dissent, and to protect himself he should insist that his dissent be recorded in the minutes.

Bylaws governing the approval cycle should make it clear that disapproval, rejection or referral back to committee for further work are available options. Procedures that ensure routine and thorough review by the full board of all committee actions will prevent committees from overriding the authority of the full board.

## EXECUTIVE COMMITTEE

The advantages of an executive committee are debated in the nonprofit world. Advocates stress the importance of continuity of organized decision making between board meetings and the need for a body to screen matters before they are submitted to the full board. Without an executive committee, the chairman alone provides interim guidance between board meetings, and important decisions may have to be delayed. An executive committee may not be necessary for the museum with a small board that meets once every month or two; but a board that meets quarterly or semiannually will likely find it difficult to function without an interim decisional body. An executive committee may assume so much power that other board members feel superfluous, however, and the board may wish to control it through bylaws specifying a rotation of membership.

The executive committee should be small, with three members the minumum number. Generally the chairman of the board is chairman of the executive committee. The authority of the executive committee has to be broad to allow for rapid action on behalf of the board, but its mandate should be written so that it clearly acts in lieu of the board's convening as often as board business needs to be transacted. Actions taken by the executive committee and all matters deliberated before it should be reported to the full board at its next meeting. They should be submitted in a form allowing the board opportunity to comment, approve and, if necessary, modify those decisions made on its behalf.

## FINANCE COMMITTEES

A standing committee for finance, budget and investment matters is a necessity for most boards, although larger institutions usually have a separate committee for each function. Institutions with substantial funds may elect a separate investment committee to monitor the performance of investment managers and in general review the institution's stewardship of funds entrusted to it. Financial matters to be reviewed by a budget committee include the total amount budgeted for staff salaries, newly established staff positions and the insurance premiums carried to cover the risks faced by the museum.

Audit is another financial concern of the board, and many organizations separate fiscal and audit functions and establish a special audit committee. The audit committee does not perform the annual audit; it recommends to the board an accounting firm to review the fiscal controls and records, and to prepare year-end financial statements. The work of the firm selected by the board is then reviewed by the audit committee, which reports the findings to the board. As the annual audit is an increasingly important responsibility of boards, members of the audit committee should have some fundamental accounting knowledge. Businessmen and accountants supportive of the museum but not members of the board might also be asked to serve. To ensure fresh insight and perspective, membership on the audit committee can be rotated.

Some museums continue to maintain a separate pension fund for employees despite the increased regulation of such funds and the penalties for noncompliance imposed by the Employee Retirement Income Security Act of 1974 (ERISA). As a result of this act, many museums have merged their former pension accounts into larger units with the requisite financial management. If the museum continues to maintain its own fund, however, the board may wish to establish a separate pension committee or a pension subcommittee of the finance committee. Those trustees who serve on such bodies will need to be familiar with the special regulatory requirements for pension fund trustees.

Boards of museums with significant fund-raising activities often appoint a separate committee on development. In some institutions this committee reviews certain solicitations and grant applications for the organization; or such review might be made by the budget committee, depending upon the museum's policies requiring board actions with respect to grants. All solicitations for funds should be made in compliance with applicable state and local laws that regulate solicitation of funds from the public.

The development committee will have to work closely with the finance or budget committee and the museum director to determine the resources that are required for planned activities. It must coordinate all its efforts with the staff development officer; indeed that officer often serves as the primary staff support for the fund-raising committee. Here relationships between employee and board official may be reversed, for the development officer is usually responsible for the execution of a grant or a capital campaign. When actually working to raise money, the committee members will have to make contacts and presentations at the direction of the development officer and keep him fully informed of all their efforts as volunteer workers, while retaining their role as overseers, policy makers and reviewers.

Museums located in sparsely populated areas may find that the only person qualified to be both treasurer and chairman of the finance committee is also an officer of the only nearby bank, and the museum will likely deposit its working capital there. In such cases the board must carefully see that the museum keeps a low cash reserve in checking and non-interest-bearing accounts, or conflict of interest charges may be leveled against the museum and its treasurer, no matter how well intentioned that trustee may be. Because of this danger, financial transactions with trustees and the firms they are associated with should be scrutinized with full understanding of the legal and reputational risks to the trustee and the museum, which will vary according to state law and the climate of public opinion in which the museum operates. The decision to proceed must be made only after full disclosure of the trustee's outside interests and the board's formal determination that the business relationship with the trustee or his organization is to the institution's clear advantage.

## COLLECTIONS MANAGEMENT COMMITTEE

The collections management responsibilities of the board are usually centered in a collections management committee, often still referred to as the acquisitions committee. The revised title connotes expanded supervision by the board of all aspects of the collection—from defining what is collected, passing upon acquisitions, setting standards for care, conservation and loan of objects and monitoring deaccessioning. For institutions that exhibit but do not own objects, a committee on loans and exhibitions fulfills the board's responsibilities to the objects under the museum's control.

The collections management committee has a particular mandate to be conversant with current legal and ethical standards applying to ethnographic material, natural history objects, live specimens and works of art protected under state or federal laws or the laws of other countries. Museums bear a special responsibility to discourage illegal traffic in artifacts, specimens or species that are endangered or represent important cultural patrimony, and the board should be aware of applicable laws and principles. Government and other organizations provide useful information on these standards and laws, and the museum's library should contain up-to-date materials.

The acquisition or disposal of museum objects requires board approval or is carried out according to procedures carefully set by the board. Loans of important objects also generally require board approval. In the procedure for deaccessioning, the museum director usually forwards the request to deaccession to the collections management committee. Some final approvals might be made at the committee level, with only a certain class of objects requiring approval by the full board. The collections management committee must exercise special care when considering the deaccession of objects that were originally accepted with legal or informal restrictions, objects that arguably should remain in some public institution or that appear to be central to the museum's purpose. In their deliberations the committee should review plans for the disposal, ensuring that the correct decisions are made and can be supported in the event of criticism. In certain instances deaccessioning can be accomplished only with the permission of the court that has jurisdiction to interpret restrictions on the museum, usually those imposed by the donor and agreed to by the museum in accepting the object.

Overseeing the museum's conservation practices is a prime responsibility of the collections management committee, for a museum has an ethical obligation to preserve and maintain what it acquires. Too often conservation has been given low budgetary priority by the board, neglected in favor of activities designed to enhance the institution's public reputation. The committee must ensure that standards for the care of objects are specifically addressed in the collections management policy and that the board allocates sufficient funds for both care and security. Insurance of the collection as part of the museum's total insurance program is another topic for the committee's agenda.

## BUILDINGS AND GROUNDS COMMITTEE

In planning for the museum's security the collections management committee will have to work closely with the buildings and grounds committee. Maintenance of the museum's physical plant is basic to the successful execution of institutional functions, and a standing committee to supervise buildings and grounds management is necessary for all but the smallest boards. That committee can recommend to the board the appropriate levels for maintenance that should be adopted as policy, suggest an insurance program covering the plant and plan for future renovations, additions and replacement of facilities. Other functions of this committee might include ensuring access for the handicapped and attention to safety laws and building ordinances. For those institutions housed in facilities constructed or maintained by a governmental unit, the buildings and grounds committee is often responsible for board liaison with the department or bureau supporting the museum's plant.

## NOMINATING COMMITTEE

The nominating committee has the central purpose of sustaining the quality of the board. In addition to its functions in carrying out the search for appropriate new members, screening prospective candidates and briefing them on their status and obligations, the committee can be responsible for orientation of all new trustees and for keeping current the board's library on trusteeship.

## OTHER COMMITTEES

Each board must determine how to organize committee assignments to achieve maximum effectiveness in its functions as policy maker and overseer for the museum's programs. The designation of the committee or committees responsible for program activities will vary according to each museum's activities. Many museums have a separate committee of the board to oversee educational and museum outreach activities. These programs are usually somewhat different in approach and philosophy from other institutional activities and so warrant a special committee made up of members who understand the educational process.

Publicizing museum activities is a separate function, and some institutions will want a committee for publicity, perhaps made up in part of outside public relations specialists. That committee's function is to watch the museum's public image and to monitor the activities that directly affect it, such as exhibitions and fund-raising events.

The salaried and volunteer staff is a valuable resource that warrants a separate committee on personnel. This committee should keep abreast of employees' legal rights and the museum's obligations under union contracts. Its members need to be conversant with current personnel management philosophies in order to review critically the staff personnel policies in use or proposed by the museum director. The committee critiques personnel management operations, including nondiscrimination and affirmative action programs, and should encourage the museum to make employment and treatment of staff as open and fair as possible. It can also hear employee grievances appealed to the board and report its recommendations to the full board for approval or modification. Because of the complexities involved when a committee serves as a court of last resort within the organization, the personnel committee and the board should always be advised by legal counsel during exercise of this function.

Some boards may want to institutionalize the planning process within a permanent planning committee. This body can work closely with the committees responsible for budgeting, investments, fund raising and buildings and grounds, and other functions requiring comprehensive advanced planning, to ensure that museum management is defining its long-term goals on a systematic basis. The committee can be the focal point for the museum's long-range strategic and financial planning, making certain that plans are updated annually, taking account of experience over the past year and projecting future trends.

Another standing assignment for a planning committee could be to monitor developments in law and legislation that affect museums. The legal posture and responsibilities of an institution are never static, for the legislated and court-made laws in every legal system tend to increase in complexity and coverage as the society it governs matures. Some larger museums have a law and planning committee to study new developments likely to affect the museum. It sees to it that measures are taken to comply and recommends ways in which the costs of compliance might be met.

# ꜩꜩ The Chairman of the Board

The bylaws generally delineate the basic responsibilities of the chairman, outlining his powers to govern the board and, through the museum director, link the board's policy making and monitoring functions to the activities of the institution. The chairman's essential duties are to preside at board meetings, initiate and coordinate board activities and be responsible for communicating to all involved parties the concerns and decisions of the board. Chairing a museum board has much in common with chairing the boards of other organizations, and those aspiring to the role can benefit greatly from the literature of chairmanship and boardmanship. But not everything can be learned from instructional texts; some aspects can be fully comprehended only through the experience of leading in a particular organizational context.

The chairman must balance conflicting interests within subunits and committees of the board, sometimes mediating between factions to maintain working harmony. He has to be alert to any cliques that exist among the trustees and to private understandings between particular members that may aim toward manipulation of the board. His is the task of controlling a trustee who attempts to dominate the board by force of will, behind-the-scenes maneuvering or sympathy appeals. These techniques disrupt the board and can cause members to withdraw from participation.

A genuine test of the chairman's executive abilities comes in his role as principal intermediary between the board and the museum director. He and the director must achieve a close working relationship, for it is the director, as the museum's chief administrative officer, who applies board policy to the actual operation of the institution. The chairman must be able to provide tactful guidance and interpretation of board action and opinion, neither offending the director's autonomy nor overstepping his own prerogatives as a representative of the board's collective authority.

A well-organized agenda is the basis of productive board meetings, and the chairman compiles the agenda, usually with the help of the museum director. The chairman also ensures that all members are apprised of meeting schedules and receive the pertinent material for study well in advance of the meeting. The agenda itself should specify which matters require board action and which are only for the trustees' information. If appropriate, the name and telephone number of the person to contact for more information about a particular matter could be included with each agenda item.

The chairman cannot turn over to the board secretary all responsibility for keeping the records documenting the board's existence and functioning; documentation is too important to delegate away. He should instruct the secretary to report to the board periodically on the system for safeguarding the minutes and records, for that material will be needed if trustees are called to account for their actions.

# ꊓꊓꊓ The Board and the Director

The board hires the director, and the director reports to the board. Since the director is responsible for the administration of board policies and all museum operations, selecting the director and establishing his working relationship with the board are among the most important actions the board takes.

The procedures for the search and selection of a museum director are similar to those used by other organizations. Often the board will appoint an *ad hoc* committee to do the necessary groundwork. The duties of the director's position need to be studied both in theory and in practice as they apply to the particular organization. The board can then prepare a position description and, from that, a list of qualifications. The director's actual performance will be measured against the position description, so the list of duties it outlines should be realistic. A manifestly unrealistic position description may discourage many candidates of ability and experience, who will recognize that the board expects the impossible.

The thought, planning and preparation necessary for hiring a new director can be used to reassess the goals, policies, operations and activities of the museum. It is a good time to consider changes in operation of the board, especially as it functions in relation to the director. If improvements are needed in carrying out existing policies and programs or if new directions should be taken, the board can seek candidates who appear capable of accomplishing these changes.

The strength and effectiveness of the relationship between the board and the director begin with an intelligently planned selection process. Seldom is the right candidate on the scene and available to fill the director's post, so public advertising and other forms of solicitation should be initiated. The solicitation and selection process must be in full compliance with applicable equal employment opportunity and affirmative action laws and policies. The scope of the solicitation is an indication of the board's interest in finding the best-qualified person. That person will have the appropriate combination of substantive knowledge of the organization's activities, management training, ability and experience.

The board may want to engage the services of a firm or individual who searches for executive talent or advises on recruitment. The firm or consultant might handle the entire process, presenting three to five individuals for final interview and selection by the board. Or the search committee may review the initial applications and place likely candidates on a short list to be interviewed. The final selection of the director is always made by the full board.

In selecting those candidates to be interviewed, the information provided by each applicant's references should be fully utilized. Applicants generally list as references only those who will give favorable reports, so checking references is frequently considered a mere formality, to be accomplished by letter if at all. But even the standard reference letter has some value; at the very least it provides a basis for pursuing discussion of a candidate's qualifications by telephone conversation. Some recruiters make it a practice to telephone a reference before deciding whether to request a written statement. At any rate, direct contact with the reference is best—either by telephone or face to face. The recruiter can then ask probing questions and request names of persons acquainted with the applicant and his work but not listed as references. Such people often provide a useful and objective assessment of the candidate's abilities. Reference checks, if conducted with intelligence and persistence, will weed out unqualified applicants, thus saving the institution time and travel expenses. The board can then concentrate on those candidates whose qualifications have been verified.

Funds should be made available to cover the travel expenses of likely candidates and to reimburse board members for expenses they incur during the selection process. It is customary to pay transportation costs for those who rate high on the basis of written applications and are selected for a personal interview. Refusal to reimburse travel expenses imposes a hardship on candidates and may turn some away. It may even be interpreted as an indication that the board will shirk other fiscal responsibilities as regards the director and the institution. No one should be invited for an interview unless the board considers him a serious candidate. Much time and energy are required for an interview, and it is unfair to involve an applicant in the process if the board is not seriously interested in him.

A small group of trustees generally carries out the final interviews. Since the potential director will get his first impression of the board during that interview, the trustees appointed to this task should be experienced in interviewing. Their objectivity is extremely important, not only in ensuring that the best candidate is selected but also in preventing favoritism from discouraging promising applicants or laying the basis for charges of discrimination.

The board should make clear what it requires of the director. Candor is recommended in discussing significant or unusual financial and other problems in the museum's operations. Most able candidates will have learned of major problems through independent investigation, so the failure to be frank can reflect on the board's forthrightness. The candidate should be told how board committees exercise their planning, policy making and overseeing functions and how much administrative assistance will be expected of him and his staff in supporting the work of board committees. The appropriate channels for communication between himself and the persons holding various board positions should be explained.

The board should expect able candidates to engage in negotiation not only over salary and benefits but also over duties and authority. In lieu of or together with a list of his duties, some candidates will ask for a contract of employment or letter of agreement specifying duties, salary and other compensation, term of service, and a standard for evaluating performance and a procedure for terminating the appointment. Written employment agreements for museum directors are becoming more common, for they provide increased definition of authority and responsibility and guarantee executives a measure of financial security over a specified period. Typically they provide for severance pay if the board wishes to terminate a director before the end of the contract period, unless he is proven to have committed malfeasance.

The museum director should expect to attend all board meetings and major committee meetings, except for executive sessions of the board when his salary or performance is being discussed. Through participation the director will gain a better sense of the board and its members; because he understands the reasoning behind board-adopted policies, he will find them easier to execute. In addition, the director will be able to provide immediate answers to questions about programs and staff, so that board members, in turn, will have a better understanding of the museum's operations.

Some directors are appointed as trustees of their institutions, but the wisdom of this practice is debated. It blurs the distinction between policy and administration, for one trustee then has a fiduciary obligation to enact policies at the same time that he must administer them. It is also argued that this practice reduces the director's answerability to the board and weakens its control of him. Then, too, the director who continues as a board member after his term expires creates a difficult circumstance for the incoming executive. The new director will inevitably want to depart from his predecessor's ways; in fact, he may have been hired to make changes. No doubt he will find the continued presence of the former director in a position of superior authority inhibiting. Knowing that the former director will be a trustee may even deter some good candidates from accepting the position. Those who favor appointing the director as a trustee believe it gives him increased stature and authority within the museum and heightens his motivation and effectiveness. In certain cases, senior museum professionals will not accept a director's position unless it includes board membership.

## WORKING WITH THE DIRECTOR

As established procedure the director should report to the board at every meeting—not necessarily in writing, because the preparation of too many written reports can consume time better spent on institutional operations, but certainly he should report informally. The director has a fundamental obligation to keep the board informed of his progress toward implementing its policies, and trustees are entitled to current and candid explanations if operations and activities do not follow the plans they have approved.

A problem for too many museums is the individual trustee who purports to give orders to the director or expresses his personal views in a manner suggesting that he expects the director to agree and alter his administrative practices accordingly. Only the chairman or other designated officer should speak for the board, and the museum's director has the right to look to the proper authority for instructions. Unless authorized to speak for the board, individual members should distinguish between their personal views and board policy in discussions with the director. Keeping the two separate prevents confusion, for the director can then weigh the merits of the statements as personal opinion and act according to their intrinsic worth. For additional discussion of the working relationship between the board and the director, see chapter II.

## EVALUATING THE DIRECTOR

The board should provide for routine review of the director's work and the museum's activities to see if board decisions are being properly executed. For this reason, a comprehensive job description against which to measure his performance is essential. The chairman is usually in the best position for informal review, for he is in frequent contact with the director and can discuss problems and progress. But a formal appraisal is also necessary. Employment agreements between many boards and executive officers specify this kind of review at stated intervals of one or two years. If the evaluation is not routinely scheduled and fully anticipated by the director and planned for by the board, it can threaten the director, and he may assume a defensive posture vis-à-vis the board. He may suspect that the evaluation is an instrument to discredit him, introduced by a faction of the trustees plotting his dismissal. Such fears are deflected if the evaluation is established as a regular procedure carried out by the full board.

The assessment is more of a learning experience when all parties are prepared and both the director and the board reach a more realistic understanding of their mutual capability for achieving their desired goals for the museum. If evaluation results are strongly negative, the full board can take appropriate action to put the director in a probationary mode or notify him of its decision to replace him. Dismissal should be considered only with full understanding of the legal rights of both board and executive. These actions must be taken only after complete deliberation by the entire board at meetings called well in advance so as many members as possible may participate. The director should be notified of board action affecting his tenure. The prudent board will consult experienced legal counsel as these situations develop, to protect both itself and its individual members from criticism, legal action and liability.

Seldom will a museum director meet all requirements set for him and his staff, and errors will be made that may elicit public criticism. Even if the alleged lapses of duty are serious or criminal, the board should be steadfast in its defense until the facts are established. Failure to give adequate support to the director and staff in the face of severe criticism may create a permanent distrust of the board that will affect working morale and eventually impair the museum's operations. When the board must assert its position in a crisis, it should appoint one spokesman so it speaks with a single voice. The other members must resist the temptation to discuss the questions with representatives of the press and public; they should refer inquiries to the trustee authorized to speak for the board.

# ⊏⊐⊏⊐⊏⊐⊏⊐⊏⊐ The Board and the Staff

The relationship between the board and the staff should be one of mutual respect based upon the staff's regard for the trustees' experience and dedication and the board's acknowledgement of the staff's technical expertise and commitment to achieving the goals of the museum. Museum board service tends to attract individuals who are deeply interested and often knowledgeable about some aspect of the institution's collections or activities. Some are strongly tempted to pursue their interests by direct interaction with pertinent staff members, but the official position a trustee holds must preclude any appearance of interference at this level of institutional operation. The relationship of staff and board members is formal, and communication with staff should be through the director or with his knowledge. When conversing with paid or volunteer staff, trustees must exercise discretion and refrain from expressing personal opinion if it seems likely to be confused with official policy or a directive from the full board. Staff members, for their part, have a professional responsibility to avoid using social occasions or chance encounters as opportunities to lobby board members for personal objectives.

# IV Accountability of Museum Trustees

The trustee's essential responsibility is the active and positive fulfillment of the trust. The trustee is answerable, or accountable, for the execution of that responsibility by his attention to the specific duties outlined in the preceding chapters, including working to establish proper policies and procedures so those obligations are carried out. Museums are receiving increasingly systematic scrutiny from various representatives of the public interest—the press, the public at large and groups within museums and the museum community, all of which claim the right to demand that trustees account for the quality of governance they give their institutions. Trustees deserve praise if responsibilities are met and tasks well done, but if responsibilities are neglected trustees can be called to account. An accounting can involve public criticism, embarrassment and actual or potential legal liability with concurrent penalties, civil or criminal. This chapter discusses the individuals, groups and government entities to which museum trustees are accountable, the reasons why these groups can challenge trustees and some of the procedures involved in responding.

## Accountability

### TO FELLOW TRUSTEES

Individual trustees are each accountable to the other board members. For centuries the law has permitted and even encouraged trustees to bring errant fellow board members to account, compelling them to justify their management of the trust before a commission of inquiry, the attorney general or a court. A charitable entity functions for the good of the public at large and has no specific beneficiaries. As a part of management, trustees are in the best position to see institutional misdirection or individual misconduct. The museum board member can bring an action against selected individual trustees or against the full board and all other members. In extreme situations a trustee may believe he has a duty to initiate legal proceedings if it appears to be the only way to correct what he considers institutional misconduct. The trustee's resort to legal action against his fellows may also be a means of protecting himself from liability, since it plainly signals his dissent. It is up to trustees to help each other carry out their responsibilities and develop adequate procedures for dealing with problem situations before any such actions become a reality.

## TO MEMBERS

In the museum that is established as a nonprofit membership organization, the trustees are elected by and accountable to the members, and members may have rights to initiate legal proceedings to correct alleged mismanagement or abuse. The legal rights of members in membership organizations or corporations to call trustees to account must be distinguished from the lesser rights of those persons who are supporting members of a museum that is not formally organized as a membership organization. Such individuals are not members in the sense that they control the organization; they are merely subscribing members of a supporting or affiliate group.

## TO STAFF

One dynamic that affects trustees is the higher level of education, training and commitment to professionalism among museum staffs. As museum directors and employees become better trained and attuned to the need for sound management practices, they will expect trustees to function with comparable attention to effective board management. The more a museum's staff expects of itself, the more it will expect of its governors. Specialists such as curators, registrars and educators have formed their own committees. These, too, urge the tightening of standards for individual museum workers and for institutional management and conduct.

## TO DONORS

A museum board is legally and ethically accountable to donors past and present; acceptance of a gift or bequest with accompanying restrictions creates an obligation that binds the museum to the perpetual enforcement of those conditions. The board should make certain that at least one of its committees has general familiarity with the terms of major gifts and bequests and access to records to allow board monitoring of the museum's conformance to all agreed-upon restrictions.

The board should also ensure that the text of each solicitation for funds is carefully examined, for the language in a solicitation can create binding obligations as to the use of the funds so raised. Careful scrutiny will avoid obligations the museum does not intend to create. The board should issue a directive to prevent informal commitments from being made as the museum solicits and accepts donations and should also be alert to statements by donors who may attempt to place moral obligations on the institution to carry out their wishes. It is customary in many museums to require donors to sign a deed of gift that transfers donations to the institution "irrevocably and unconditionally." This procedure makes it clear that the museum accepts the objects without restrictions or conditions.

If there is doubt concerning the museum's obligations or whether it did agree to certain conditions, donors or their heirs may attempt to force the institution to comply with alleged or actual restrictions and promises as to the use and disposition of particular gifts. Frequently donors are not allowed to enforce restrictions in their own name, but if they are denied direct access to the courts they can attempt to persuade the attorney general to sue. Only if he determines it appropriate will suit be brought, for as a general rule members of the public cannot force the attorney general to act. Although these legal actions are filed against the museum as an entity, trustees can be sued as individual defendants because of their role as ultimate guarantors of the institution's promises. The trustees must defend their participation in the matters raised, though personal liability seldom results unless mismanagement by the board is proven.

## TO ARTISTS

The European concept of *droit moral*—the right of the artist to have a continuing interest in the treatment of his creation—is gaining support in the United States. A California statute recognizes artists' rights, and similar legislation has been proposed in other states. Such legislation acknowledges the artist's right to secure his work against defacement or alterations that would compromise its essential integrity. Museum boards should seek to understand the current ethical force of the concept of *droit moral*, for it will be the basis for moral challenges to museums and their policies covering display, conservation and the concomitant respectful care of works of art. In those jurisdictions that adopt *droit moral*, or "art preservation," legislation, the philosophical challenges of the artist will have the force of law.

## TO GROUPS WITH AN INTEREST IN MUSEUMS

Because the museum board and its trustees carry out the specific purposes and traditions of museums as tax-exempt public institutions, they are accountable to all persons and groups with an interest in museums. The American Association of Museums has been the principal organized group speaking for the museum community in the United States since the beginning of the present century. The AAM has many constituent units or committees concerned with particular types of institutions, such as youth and science museums, and comprised of specialists, including curators, educators, registrars and security personnel. Canada and Great Britain have associations representing their museums, and the International Council of Museums is concerned with museums worldwide. Museum associations and their constituent units have an interest in the standards by which particular museums are managed, for whatever is done in one museum inevitably reflects upon all.

There are other organizations that represent particular types of museums in the United States. The American Association for State and Local History has a constituency of several thousand historical organizations. The Association of Science and Technology Centers speaks for the interests of those institutions that exhibit the principles and application of scientific discoveries. The Association of Art Museum Directors is especially concerned with the management and ethical practices of art museums. The

American Association of Zoological Parks and Aquariums and the American Association of Botanical Gardens and Arboreta serve the specialized interests of those institutions.

The accreditation program of the American Association of Museums sets basic standards for a museum board's organization and operation, and boards of accredited museums must continue to operate within the limits set by those standards. They are described in *Professional Standards for Museum Accreditation.* Those obligations for museum trustees set forth in *Museum Ethics* were adopted in 1978 as the standard of conduct and code of ethics for institutional and individual members of the AAM. Standards for trustee responsibility and management within the museum field will continue to evolve, and the board must keep abreast of them.

## TO GROUPS CLAIMING CULTURAL PATRIMONY

As an institution holding in trust objects important for future generations, the museum should be prepared to respond to interests concerned with the preservation of cultural traditions. Collections management and in particular conservation policies adopted by the board will be scrutinized, and if objects of concern to special groups are not properly conserved, those groups will protest. Other groups may insist on special standards for the maintenance of objects important to them. American Indian tribes, for example, may insist that certain objects be stored or displayed only in accordance with the ceremonial precedents of their tribes.

In some cases demands will be made for museums to transfer some of their holdings, either permanently or on long-term loan, to other nations and cultural subunits claiming cultural patrimony. The basis for these demands may be that the objects were looted in times past or are so vital to the continuation of a culture that the museum has a moral obligation to accede. These demands can require complex negotiations and imaginative solutions. A museum's involvement in such questions can be minimized, however, by the board's insistence upon knowing the immediate origin and provenance, or history of ownership, of objects proposed as accessions and its firm refusal of objects whose provenance is doubtful.

## TO THE PUBLIC AT LARGE

Museum boards should realize that with heightened visibility and attention comes the increased concern of a broadened constituency. As the governing body, the board has an obligation to respond to legitimate inquiry openly and honestly, even in areas of potential embarrassment. The public has the right to be reassured as to the proper functioning of its institutions, and the board can do much to preclude further controversy by a direct and forthright response.

The museum board that is open and responsive to inquiries may thereby avoid being compelled to answer those questions in a lawsuit. Inquirers are sometimes able to make legally enforceable demands. Suit can be prosecuted only by individuals with a legal interest, or "standing to sue," but courts are frequently lenient in finding the requisite legal interest if it appears that the litigants will perform a public service by bringing a particular situation to light. Certain members of the public may be allowed to prosecute their claim of negligence or malfeasance on the theory that the incumbents are mismanaging the organization. In many jurisdictions these public interest plaintiffs may be joined by the state attorney general. If the suit is successful, the court may award the plaintiffs reasonable fees for their attorneys' services, charging such costs against the charitable entity. In rare cases board members might be held personally liable for the plaintiffs' costs and attorneys' fees.

## TO THE STATE AND THE COURTS

The common institutional sentinel for museums is the state attorney general. In nearly every state, by either statute or common law principles, the attorney general has oversight powers over museums and all other educational and public service organizations. His office oversees the array of public charities in an effort to keep them true to their purposes and efficient in their use of the resources under their control. Usually the charities division of an attorney general's office has time actively to investigate only cases of suspected or reported abuse, but it has the power to make inquiry of any organization under its jurisdiction and to demand a response.

States normally require nonprofit organizations to file annual reports summarizing the financial aspects of their operations and a list of names and addresses of current trustees and officers. Museum trustees must ensure that these state reports are submitted each year. Failure to file can signal either defunct status or misappropriation of assets, triggering inquiry or investigation.

Institutions holding collections receive particular attention from state officials because objects under the care of museums are viewed as cultural resources belonging to the people. All aspects of collections management policy and practice will interest state overseers, but their role as protectors of the public's treasures will be most active when a museum deaccessions or disposes of objects in its collections. If the museum sells or trades to another museum or public service institution and the objects remain available to the public for study and use, scrutiny is usually less intense. But officials in certain states may still severely question such transactions if the objects are to be transferred to an institution in another state.

The prudent museum board will be aware of prevailing attitudes toward deaccessioning within its state's hierarchy and will make certain that all appropriate policies and procedures are in effect before disposing of any object. The review procedures and safeguards should increase for objects above certain dollar values or for items of particular historic, cultural or scientific merit. Some museum boards will find it practical to consult the appropriate state officials at the time the museum plans the disposal of any substantial object or portion of its collection. The state will hold the board accountable for what it views as improper disposal.

Museum boards also function under the aegis of the court system, although normally it is the attorney general who calls trustees to account before a judge. English courts have enforced the obligations of trustees of charities since the 1400s, and that oversight jurisdiction continues in the United States. Courts are not active overseers as are attorneys general, but once the affairs of an institution are brought before a court, by either citizen-plaintiffs or the attorney general, the court can retain oversight jurisdiction. This continuing power enables the court to direct the organization's management in carrying out all aspects of its decree. The original plaintiffs or their representatives may easily reactivate judicial scrutiny by petitioning the court.

The board must be prepared to answer for the museum's record of compliance with employment discrimination statutes,

wage and hour laws, occupational safety and health acts, charitable solicitation legislation and other regulatory provisions, even
though such requirements are imposed directly on the institution.
Traditionally it has been the museum director and his staff who
have been held to account for compliance in these areas, but
board members could be accountable if they approved a policy
or took an action patently contrary to law.

## TO THE FEDERAL GOVERNMENT

When discharging its responsibility to protect the museum's
preferred tax status, the board should be sensitive to the functions
of the Internal Revenue Service (IRS). Federal tax authorities not
only certify charities as tax exempt; they also oversee the finances
of nonprofit organizations to ensure that they continue to qualify
for whatever status has been granted.

The Internal Revenue Service also guards against practices of
tax-exempt organizations that aid the unlawful reduction of taxes
due from private individuals and organizations and other abuses
resulting in improper profits or unlawful private gain. Trustees
can be held accountable if they sanction such practices. The
museum must file a financial report with the IRS each year, and
the board should make certain that the report is prepared by or
with the assistance of an accountant experienced in nonprofit
accounting. He will be familiar with current accounting standards
and IRS guidelines and will be able to complete the form so as
to meet IRS standards and retain for the museum the most
favorable tax-exempt classification possible. If the museum fails
to file its information reports with the IRS, penalties can be
imposed upon the officers or trustees who have the responsibility
for filing them.

The board must also see that the institution makes proper
payment to the IRS of taxes withheld from employees' salaries.
Officials of organizations, including trustees of nonprofit entities,
could be held personally liable for amounts due, plus penalties,
if the organization fails to remit payments. To ensure that the
total amount due to the government is on hand at all times, taxes
withheld from employees and the requisite employer contributions can be paid into a special trust account.

Government grants that constitute a substantial amount of the
museum's budget should be approved by the board or accepted

by staff according to guidelines set by the board. In providing for acceptance of grants or in approving the receipt of individual grants, the board should ensure that the terms certified to as conditions of awards can be carried out. For example, if a grant requires certification of an affirmative action plan for the employment of minorities, the board should make sure there is an adequate plan. The board's complicity in a misleading certification could cause trustees to be required to answer to government grantors.

A board might also be directly accountable if it sanctions management and accounting practices that allow funds granted for a specified purpose to be used by the museum for another activity. Here the board could be implicated in misspending grant funds and might be held accountable for unauthorized expenditures, especially if the monies are federal.

## SPECIAL ACCOUNTABILITY
## OF THE GOVERNMENT MUSEUM

For many museums with close affiliations to the federal or a state or local government, certain kinds of accountability are provided for by legislation. Statutes or ordinances may dictate that the records pertaining to the museum and its board are public documents and must be furnished to any person who files a request according to procedures outlined in the law. These freedom of information statutes allow certain categories of documents to be withheld, such as employee personnel files and other information given the organization in confidence, but the museum may have a heavy legal burden to justify withholding most records. If the request is for information not clearly protected by an exception, it is usually best to release the documents. The possibility of public disclosure of documents should be a strong incentive for boards of government museums to maintain records of their activities that prove their members are meeting their responsibilities.

Legislation that may apply to government museums in some jurisdictions requires meetings to be open to the public. The definition of "meeting" in these so-called sunshine laws may be so inclusive that a discussion of museum business among three or more trustees cannot be held except in compliance with the proper notice and other procedures specified in the law. The museum board subject to open-meeting legislation must consult with its legal counsel and adopt rules for its meetings that conform to the law. Most boards have not found that the occasional public observer is a substantial impediment to effective deliberation and action. Museums not subject to sunshine laws can continue to hold traditional closed board meetings.

Special fiscal regulations apply to the museum supported from a government treasury. Trustees need not master the details of these financial laws but should be mindful of their general principles and application, so that budgeting and spending policies set by the board conform to that government's fiscal universe.

# ᴣᴦᴣᴦᴣᴦ Responding to Inquiries

Public relations functions for a museum board should be adequately organized to permit ready answer to questions from the press and the public. When necessary, emergency meetings of the public relations committee, the executive committee or even the full board may be warranted to decide upon the appropriate response. Well-drafted bylaws will provide for these special meetings.

If the board can produce all the data relevant to an inquiry and make a clear and honest response to the questions raised, most critics will be satisfied. The response is often particularly effective when it includes records prepared in the ordinary course of business, for these records are proof that the board routinely discharges its responsibilities. Rarely should an inquiry be ignored, and certainly the board cannot afford to decide whether or not to respond according to the degree of embarrassment it might suffer if it answers. It is preferable to be slightly embarrassed at the outset of an inquiry than to let the matter fester until it becomes a full-blown scandal. If a spokesman for the board is selected, he should be a person who can be trusted to respond in a candid, factual manner without appearing defensive.

Museums are often asked for information about donors, donations and acquisitions when they have good reasons to remain silent. Donors may demand anonymity, or negotiations prior to an acquisition may be sensitive. Thus the board should anticipate questions to which it cannot respond by full disclosure and adopt a policy and procedures to explain the institution's response. If the museum is subject to a freedom of information or public disclosure act, a detailed written opinion of counsel should be obtained to ascertain which records must be released and which may be withheld. Armed with this opinion, the museum can advise donors of the level of confidentiality it is allowed to maintain, so that it makes no promises which cannot legally be kept.

Boards should be aware that most public disclosure acts do not require the questioner to provide any reason whatsoever for demanding information. The theory of such legislation is that the information is in the public domain and therefore available to anyone on demand. Those who speak for nongovernmental public service organizations should likewise not refuse reputable inquirers information with the comment that they have no reason to know. This response may well provoke indignation and escalate a simple question into a major investigation.

# V Liabilities of Museum Trustees

The status of trusteeship contains inherent liability because the trust obligation is assumed even though service is voluntary. The trustee who fails to meet his responsibilities can be held accountable in a legal proceeding in which it can be decreed that he must make personal reparation for losses sustained by the organization from his lapses of duty. The potential for being sued or for incurring liability, however, will be greatly decreased if appropriate precautions are scrupulously observed by both boards and individual trustees. Thoughtful application of the principles discussed in this handbook and careful attention to the details of sound management are the surest protection against suit or liability of any sort.

Trustees and their attorneys should also be aware that there are very few cases involving museums that have been brought to a final judgment by a court. Theories for trustee liability have been alleged in several complaints filed in recent years by attorneys general, but their theories and assertions have usually been ruled neither valid nor invalid because the proceedings did not reach the stage where the allegations of trustee liability were accepted or approved in a judge's statement or a court decree. Such assertions by attorneys general are useful, however, in predicting the kinds of situations most likely to get trustees involved in litigation and to steer them away from possible lawsuits and potential liability. This handbook attempts to alert trustees and their lawyers to the areas in which further challenges to boards, to individual trustees and to museums might be anticipated in the years immediately ahead.

Despite potential and threatened liability, as of the time this handbook goes to press no court has entered a monetary

ent against a museum trustee, although a few trustees have
_ bear the expense of retaining personal legal counsel.
Some of the suits against museum board members that are
pending could result in liability when concluded, whether by a
judgment of the court or an agreed-upon settlement. Litigation
can go on for five or even ten years, so a favorable judgment or
settlement may be at best a Pyrrhic victory for the board and the
individual trustees sued. Some legal actions brought to a conclusion favorable to the trustees act as deterrents to further challenges to that board and its members and can discourage similar
litigation against other organizations. The extent to which a suit
won by trustees of one institution deters other litigation depends
upon whether the organizations are in the same state and the
strength of the legal reasoning and precedent that contributed
to the trustees' success.

A distinction must be made between legal actions that attempt
to impose personal liability on board members and suits filed
against museums that challenge the right or the power of a
museum and its board to take certain actions as an institution.
Trustees are frequently named as defendants in these lawsuits,
and often the board must assist in defending the institution's
course of conduct and its power to act. Such challenges, however,
seldom have any potential for the trustee's personal loss or
liability, unless they are accompanied by allegations of trustee
mismanagement or misconduct.

# ⫘⫘⫘⫘⫘ Liability for Collections Management

Most of the cases in which museum boards and individual trustees
have been brought to litigation and threatened with personal
liability have focused on mismanagement of collections or improper personal dealings with respect to the museum's objects.
Suit is frequently triggered by disposal of collection objects, for
deaccessioning invites scrutiny of a museum and its management.
Liability would be expected in this area because the cultural
importance of museum artifacts can be supported by legal theory,
which holds the boards of those institutions owning collections

to the highest of fiduciary standards. Museum boards can be considered as trustees for society of those objects within their institutions and consequently personally liable for negligence, mismanagement or self-dealing with respect to the collections.

Legal proceedings were instigated against the trustees of one museum that neglected its responsibility for collections management, by default delegating to the museum director authority to sell and trade collection items. The director engaged in questionable transactions, including alleged sales or trades of museum objects to trustees. Records of the collection were inadequate, and in the course of litigation the museum agreed to complete an inventory. This litigation was filed by the state attorney general following a complaint by a dissident trustee and sought personal judgments against the trustees for alleged neglect of duties. The attorney general retained detailed oversight of that museum's management and its board for several years, pending the reorganization of the board and the museum's administration and completion of the inventory. During this time the attorney general also had special powers to control any disposals from the collections. In 1980, after five years of oversight of the museum's practices, the museum as an entity was dismissed as a defendant in the litigation. However, those individuals who were trustees of the museum at the time of the practices complained of remain defendants in the pending legal action, with the potential for personal liability.

In another case suit was brought by the attorney general alleging personal liability of the trustees of a museum on the grounds that poor management by the board caused the collections to decline in value. It was charged that the board had for many years kept in office a director who was not trained to understand the value of the museum's objects. He allowed the objects to deteriorate. Moreover, he sold and traded items without regard for the integrity of the collection and virtually without guidance from the board. A replacement director hired by the board also mismanaged the collections. After protracted investigation and negotiations, the suit was dismissed without liability to individual trustees when the board agreed to proceed legally against the replacement director.

Another case against museum trustees, still in litigation, involves alleged neglect of the collections, including deterioration, failure to display the objects for public viewing and sales of objects that should have remained in the museum. According to the attorney general's complaint, the proceeds of these sales, which in most museums are used to acquire other objects, were designated to make up operating deficits incurred by payment of excessive salaries to the museum director and other officers. Some of those salaried officers also were trustees. The attorney general asserted in the suit that the members of the board of this nonprofit corporation were trustees of the collection for the benefit of the public. This litigation set in motion an investigation of all museums in the state by a committee of the legislature.

Another case of alleged self-dealing by a trustee arose from his use of the museum for the storage, maintenance and restoration of a number of large objects in his personal collection. The trustee, who was president of the museum and a member of the board for part of the period involved, continually promised that the objects in the custody of the museum would be donated to it. Based upon those promises the museum spent many thousands of dollars for special storage facilities and additional thousands of hours of time in maintenance and restoration of the objects. After he left the board, the former trustee attempted to sell some of the items, and when the buyers tried to remove them from the museum's premises the museum obtained a court order prohibiting their removal. The matter was settled when the former trustee donated the objects to the museum.

Relevant to the question of personal liability of trustees is an action to recover over two million dollars that has been pending for the last several years against a museum curator for alleged improper trading of collection objects with a dealer. The objects traded apparently escalated very rapidly in value, and within several weeks after the museum traded, a number of them were appraised at many times the barter prices. The objects had been appraised prior to the trades, but the attorney general alleges a conspiracy among the curator, the appraiser and the dealer to defraud the museum of its collections. The curator did have previous personal transactions with the dealer, who had purchased objects from the curator's personal collection, and the attorney general alleges that the curator made improper profits from those sales. The museum's trustees, who have not been brought into the litigation even though they formally approved the transactions, asserted that they relied completely on the curator's expertise when they voted to approve the trades.

The attorney general's theory for prosecution is that the curator was a trustee of the collections and thus should be held to the highest fiduciary standard, and in particular he should have disclosed to the museum his personal financial relationship with the dealer. A trustee may be charged with a breach of trust if he has personal dealings with the same business or individual he deals with as trustee for the trust when he appears to be making a profit because of his position as trustee and he does not disclose that he is dealing both as trustee and for himself. If strict trustee rules can be imposed upon curators, it is certain they will be applied to boards and to individual members in situations where board actions or those of individual trustees might represent dereliction of duty to the objects entrusted to the museum.

# ⸦⸧⸦⸧ Liability for Acquisitions

The liabilities of museum trustees as regards acquisition of collections have remained latent. To date only commercial dealers and a few employees have been in actual litigation or threatened with suit resulting from the acquisition of objects, specimens or endangered species under questionable circumstances. The laws constituting this network of potential liability include foreign and domestic customs laws and legislation designed to restrict or prohibit the removal from place of origin of archeological objects, biological specimens, protected live animals and national treasures. This mosaic of law is enforced by both civil and criminal penalties.

There are also provisions relating to this network of laws in national constitutions, treaties among nations and a multilateral convention agreed upon in 1970 by representatives of many countries meeting under the auspices of the United Nations Educational, Scientific, and Cultural Organization (UNESCO). Most of the nations importing objects in the categories covered by that document, including the United States, have not as yet effectuated the UNESCO convention by enacting the legislation required for implementation.

Enforcement authorities, therefore, are exercising great determination and ingenuity in the use of existing laws to attempt to halt the traffic in irreplaceable biological and cultural materials. Museums and zoos are logical repositories for these materials, so their acquisitions will no doubt receive increased scrutiny in the future. If trustees authorize the acquisition of an art or archeological object or natural specimen of questionable origin when they are cognizant, or should be, that trafficking in such items might be illegal, they are moving uncomfortably close to possible prosecution. The regulatory legislation in this area applies to anyone who receives, transfers or is implicated in the receipt or acquisition of protected objects or specimens.

Museums cannot assume they are exempt as a target of law enforcement because they operate for the public good and not for profit. Indeed, they are prime candidates for investigation and prosecution because in past years they have acquired so much material that would now be contraband. The board should draft the museum's collections management policy with full comprehension of the laws applying to the kinds of objects collected and ascertain that the registrar and other staff members receive current information about those areas of the law applicable to the museum's collections.

# Liability for Conflicts of Interest

Conflicts of interest constitute an expanding area for possible criticism and embarrassment as well as for increasing potential liability for museum trustees. Accusations of conflict of interest against trustees greatly outnumber the instances in which liability has actually been imposed, although successful defense when a conflict is alleged can be time consuming and expensive. Defense costs may or may not be payable by the museum, depending upon the precise facts of the conflict of interest as assessed by applicable state law and the ability of the museum to indemnify. Indemnification and insurance protection are discussed in detail at the end of this chapter.

Almost every person active in the business or public service sectors of community life has potential or actual conflicts of interests, and at some point in every trustee's tenure on the board he may have obligations or commitments incompatible with his responsibilities to the museum. It is most important that trustees understand conflicts of interest. If trustees recognize and acknowledge conflicts in a timely manner, situations can usually be managed so that criticism is minimized and liability avoided. The board and counsel can assist trustees in coping with whatever incompatibilities exist between their board obligations and their other personal and professional interests and commitments. Typical remedial measures are disclosure or insulation of personal interests from board obligations and actions.

Severe conflicts of interest that disable board service—such as the professional activities of a dealer or appraiser of museum objects—should be identified before the selection of candidates for board membership. The effective nominating committee will be alert to potential conflicts and discuss them openly with the persons they are considering. If a conflict appears to be uncontainable in relation to board service, candidacy is often dropped by mutual agreement. However, a conflict between a member's board service and his outside commitments may arise at any time during his tenure, and each trustee needs to be educated to recognize potential problems as they occur.

## COLLECTING OBJECTS RELATED TO THE MUSEUM'S COLLECTIONS

Conflicts of interest involving trustees who collect objects similar to those held by the museum are common problems for museum boards. Collectors are both sought after and attracted to board service because they have knowledge of and interest in the museum's collecting goals and may donate pieces to the museum from their personal holdings. This kind of conflict of interest is manageable, however, unless a collector is so active as to be classified as a dealer.

A basic tenet for the fiduciary is that he may not compete with the object of his trust. Thus the trustee's own acquisitions must not compete with his museum's; he is obligated to put the collecting ambitions of his institution before his own. The collections management policy should itemize in detail the collecting interests of the museum so that trustees who collect are put on notice that certain activities related to their personal collecting must be circumscribed while they serve on the board. The policy ought to prescribe what should be done in the event that a trustee purchases a piece he knows is of interest to the museum. He might, for example, be expected to offer it to the museum at the price he paid or to give the museum the chance to acquire it when funds can be allocated for the purchase. The ethical standards that the board adopts for managing potential conflicts of interest for trustees are, in some museums, the same as those applied to the staff. The rules for staff with respect to collecting generally aim to prevent situations in which staff members compete with the museum or profit from their positions or official duties.

A statement from the trustee who collects objects similar to those held and acquired by the museum, describing generally his personal collection and his collecting ambitions, is an important step in managing this conflict of interest. This statement should be submitted to the board in writing when the trustee is elected to membership. It will provide the board with the information it needs to structure the trustee's board participation for the maximum use of his knowledge and abilities and the minimum potential embarrassment or liability to him and to the museum.

Trustees who are collectors should not make up a majority of the collections management committee because they will have to abstain from participation when the committee is considering the acquisition or exhibition of objects similar to those in their personal collections. The trustee who collects could be liable to the museum for profits he makes as a provable consequence of actions taken by the museum if his participation was a major influence in the institution's decision to take those actions. Such a case might occur, for example, if he persuaded the museum to hold an exhibition of objects represented in his personal collection and then was able to sell those objects at a profit. Whether his objects were exhibited or not, there is a conflict of interest and potential liability to the museum in this situation.

Trustees should be especially aware of the conflict of interest hazards in personally acquiring objects from the museum's collections. This is the kind of deaccessioning practice most likely to attract the attorney general's attention and the severe criticism of groups concerned about the museum's integrity. Some insti-

"The Museum Trustee's ultimate responsibility to his museum is to ensure through his active and affirmative guidance that his institution's resources are prudently and efficiently managed to serve its purposes.

The law imposes liability upon the trustee if he fails in the fulfillment of his obligation."

MUSEUM TRUSTEESHIP

by Alan D. & Patricia Ullberg, 1981

-fundraising
-investment and cash management
-lobbying governments

* The Board must hire the C.E.O. and establish personnel policies.

* The Board must evaluate museum operations.

* The Board must self-manage in such a way as to avoid manipulation.

* The Board must establish a "Code of Ethics" or "Conduct" to guide the conduct of all members of the organization, including the trustees.

tutions include in their collections management policy a total prohibition against trustees or staff acquiring from the collections, even at public auction. A well-advertised public sale is the minimum necessary insulation for the trustee (or even a member of his family) who acquires an object from the museum. Not even public auction, however, will protect the trustee who is alleged to have obtained from his official position proprietary information that facilitated his purchase of museum objects because he knew more than the other bidders. If there appeared to be abuse of inside information, a court might order profits made on a subsequent sale to be transferred to the museum. The trustee who acquires directly from the museum's collections is inviting a lawsuit in which he might be required either to return the purchase to the museum or to pay the institution all profits from a resale.

## SELLING PRODUCTS AND SERVICES TO THE MUSEUM

An all-too-frequent conflict of interest is represented by the board member who sells goods or services to the museum. The situation is difficult to manage at best, for, even if the institution clearly benefits from the arrangement, the appearance of advantage to the trustee may cause embarrassment to both the institution and the trustee. In addition, such an arrangement, once entered into, is difficult to break without hard feelings. In effect, it often limits the museum. Every institution should maintain as much autonomy as possible in selecting and changing suppliers of goods and services, to get the best possible product at the lowest possible price. The museum's ability to demand the highest quality product can be impaired if a trustee is the supplier, for members of the board may find it difficult to exercise a supervisory role over their peers.

Personal monetary liability can be imposed on the trustee who sells to the museum if he overcharges or provides materials or services of poor quality. Regardless of the value he gives, he is vulnerable to charges because he is a member of the board. The trustee and board must always be prepared to demonstrate that the goods or services were both necessary and satisfactorily delivered and that the prices were reasonable. This burden of proof may be difficult to carry in every situation, for the presumption will be that favoritism is the basis for the business relationship.

It is a fundamental duty of a fiduciary to disclose all conflicting or adverse interests. In the absence of full disclosure, actual monetary liability can be created for the trustee who sells to his institution through an intermediary or through a firm in which he owns a significant interest. If challenged in court, the minimum the trustee must prove is that the museum was not harmed financially. In some jurisdictions the trustee could be liable for profits from the transaction even if the museum receives full value. A trustee who fails to disclose interests adverse to his trust can be required to relinquish any gain from such dealings. These principles generally do not apply to the trustee who owns a small percentage of shares in a company and takes no part in its management and so is unaware it might be a supplier to the museum. He can still be criticized, however, so it is prudent for trustees to ascertain if companies in which they hold equity interests deal with the museum.

One situation deserving special comment is that of the trustee who is a lawyer and serves as paid counsel for the institution. Attorneys can be valuable board members, assisting with procedural snarls during meetings, giving advice on general legal questions, drafting bylaws and resolutions and executing other routine tasks where legal training is an advantage. But there is some question whether it is prudent practice for the board to engage a trustee or his law firm to carry out defined legal tasks for which he expects to be paid. Any such assignment has all the problems of the situation in which a trustee supplies goods to the institution. The arrangement is more open to question if the trustee or his firm is retained to defend or prosecute an action that develops out of business before the board in which he participated as a member, for the trustee is then involved as both board member and attorney. An attorney's obligation is to provide the best, most objective legal advice he can, and if he is involved as both substantive decision maker and attorney-adviser, he may not be able to remain entirely objective. Nor can objectivity be assured if the trustee simply assigns the matter to an associate in his law firm, for the associate may be reluctant to suggest that a senior member of the firm made errors in judgment or that the board is at fault in the matter. If the matter could involve liability on his part, the wise lawyer-trustee will step aside and make certain he and other board members are represented by an attorney or firm that has no ties to the museum. Some law firms have a policy of declining to serve as counsel in any legal matter that might involve liability on the part of a board member who is associated with the firm.

Liability can also grow out of the situation of the board member supplying investment services to the museum, though the laws pertaining to such matters vary from state to state. As the result of his taking charge of the institution's portfolio, a trustee associated with an investment firm can easily be placed in a position the law could view as divided loyalty. The law may require the fiduciary who mingles trust and personal business to make good any losses to the trust, even if there is no provable connection between the trustee's personal dealings and the losses sustained by the trust. This requirement is a time-honored rule to discourage trustees from tempting situations.

## OTHER CONFLICTS OF INTEREST

As planners, policy makers and overseers of the museum, trustees are exposed to much proprietary information. Prices paid for acquisitions, long-range plans for exhibitions and restricted data about financial matters are examples of the knowledge available only to insiders. Board members have ethical and legal obligations to refrain from utilizing proprietary information for their personal gain or that of close associates. On occasion a trustee may be compelled to pay to the organization the profits he gained through the exploitation of information to which he had access as an individual privy to the entity and its sources of information, for the courts are quick to penalize the official who gains improper advantage from his position. Liability of a trustee for abuse of inside information is not based on the extent of harm to the entity but is imposed to uphold the rigid standard prohibiting a fiduciary from profiting from his trust. If a trustee is in doubt as to the propriety of using for personal purposes information gained through his participation as a board member, the question should be discussed with the chairman of the board and with an attorney who understands the workings of the museum and the legal limits on the use of information by insiders.

Conflicts of interest that develop from board members' personal dedication to the welfare and support of other organizations seldom lead to monetary liability. These are situations of multiple loyalties, which can generally coexist so long as the trustee makes full disclosure of all other positions he holds and refrains from attempting to use his position in one organization for the benefit of any other. Courts are swift to order the removal of trustees who participate in actions that might assist other organizations in which they hold office or to which they have a demonstrated commitment. Court-ordered removal from a board is not a monetary loss, but it is an embarrassment to all concerned: the individual member who deliberately or innocently participated, the organization that allowed him to participate and the outside entity that was the presumed beneficiary of the trustee's technical breach of loyalty. A monetary liability would be imposed only if it could be proved that the trustee deliberately tried to use the museum's assets or reputation to benefit the other organization and that the museum sustained a measurable monetary loss in the process. It is possible that the trustee might be ordered to make up such a loss. Some boards make it a policy to exclude from candidacy individuals who are trustees of certain other nonprofit institutions.

It is instructive to contrast conflicts of interest to situations in which trustees abuse their position by demanding special privileges. A conflict of interest places the trustee in a position in which a financial tie or an attachment to a definite personal goal or to another organization is antagonistic to his duty of loyalty to the museum. Abuse of position is a simple overreaching for general selfish purposes. The use of museum property or staff resources to execute personal business are examples. Board members should not request staff assistance for personal projects; it is difficult for staff to refuse, but they inevitably resent the request and lose respect for the trustee. Trustees should not expect to have a special personal claim on use of museum resources, and a case of proven abuse could force repayment to the institution for the value of that appropriated. Extreme cases of special privilege can lead to loss of the museum's tax exemption. A basic condition for tax-exempt status is that the resources of the organization not be used for the benefit of or inure to any private individual.

## PROTECTION FROM LIABILITY
## FOR CONFLICT OF INTEREST

The best protection from liability for conflict of interest is full disclosure of outside interests that might be relevant to service for the museum. Disclosure should begin before trustees are nominated to the board. Conflicts of interest that are disabling should lead to a withdrawal from candidacy; for those conflicts that can be managed, guidelines regarding the candidate's board participation can be laid down. In some states the disclosure statements filed by board members of government museums are public documents. This condition of board service must be explained to candidates in the preliminary interview, so that those who object can withdraw from candidacy.

Once they are on the board, trustees should file disclosure statements every year. These annual disclosure statements ought to be in a form prescribed by the board so that information relevant to the museum's activities is obtained and all trustees disclose their interests according to the same criteria. Museums may find it helpful to give their board members a list of the organizations engaged in significant transactions with the institution so that the trustees can make accurate statements concerning their relationships to them. The disclosure statements should be reviewed by the chairman or an appropriate representative of the board, and, where necessary, the data can be supplemented by discussions with those members whose statements raised questions. The statements should be kept in the confidential custody of the board chairman or the designated committee.

In addition, a disclosure should be made at any time during a trustee's tenure when a specific matter involving his outside interests could affect his participation as a board member. These *ad hoc* disclosure statements should be noted in the board's records, and the minutes should reflect whether the board deemed mere disclosure of the interest sufficient or that protective action was taken.

Protective action will usually entail the trustee's abstention from voting or other participation in pertinent board actions. Abstention from voting as a board member serves as complete protection from liability for most conflict of interest situations. In some states the interested trustee must refrain from voting, for if he votes the board's action is not valid. There are situations in which it is also prudent for the trustee to refrain from discussing or even attending that portion of the meeting that involves an issue closely affecting his personal interests. By these means the board can protect itself and the individual trustee from embarrassment and possible liability from conflicts of interest.

# ൰൰൰൰൰൰൰൰൰ Fiscal Liabilities

The liabilities of museum boards that develop from their answerability for the fiscal management of their institutions are similar to those in other nonprofit organizations. The probability of suffering an adverse judgment in litigation will depend upon the particular form and degree of mismanagement, measured against those laws of the jurisdiction that apply to financial fiduciaries. Law varies from state to state, but the principles for imposing liabilities upon trustees for institutional mismanagement are generally observed in all jurisdictions.

The cases involving museum trustees in litigation over fiscal assets were precipitated, by and large, by an alleged scandal concerning the collections; once investigation was initiated, various points of alleged fiscal negligence were added to the charges. One museum's collections deteriorated seriously, partly because of generally lax financial controls but also through neglect of the buildings. In addition, income property belonging to the museum and leased to a board member was the object of board action allegedly favorable to that trustee. The case was settled without liability to any trustee; the museum's director was alleged to be the party responsible for the harm to the museum and its assets.

Another museum put most of its collection into storage and rarely opened its doors to the public. Despite minimal activity and decreasing revenues, the board authorized substantial salaries to staff officers, some of whom were trustees of the museum. To cover operating losses the board authorized sales at auction of significant objects from the collection. The attorney general filed suit after his investigation revealed that the board also sanctioned use of institutional financial assets for a board member's private business ventures. This case is still in litigation, although the attorney general was successful in obtaining a court injunction to halt some of the planned sales of the museum's objects.

A form of irresponsible fiscal management that can incur liability is authorization by the board of purchases or other financial commitments when it has no reasonable assurance or expectation that the institution can meet the obligation. A major purpose of the corporate or trust form of organization for a nonprofit entity is to insulate managers—including board members—from personal liability for the acts and obligations of the entity. But if that privilege of limited liability is abused by ordering goods or services when there is no expectation that they can be paid for, the board is participating in a fraud upon the supplier. If the organization placing the order is insolvent and cannot expect to meet its commitments soon or within a reasonable time, the members of the board might be compelled to pay the creditors from their personal funds. Only in extreme situations would trustees be held liable, but if the board does not ensure that revenues are reasonably adequate to meet obligations, the threat of legal action is there.

Federal income tax statutes may also entail liability for museum trustees. The government has obtained a personal judgment against the chairman of the board of at least one nonprofit corporation because of the organization's failure to pay employees' withholding taxes to the Internal Revenue Service. If these taxes cannot be paid by the organization or its managers who are immediately responsible, an assessment can be made against the officers of the board or any individual member. A trustee could be personally liable for the full amount of the unpaid withholding taxes and for the interest and statutory penalties. The board can avoid any liability of this nature by insistence on full funding on a current basis in a special trust account of all taxes due and by monitoring that account and the payment of withholding taxes. Special taxes and penalties can be imposed upon those who are trustees of museums classified as private operating foundations if such trustees engage in acts of self-dealing as defined by the applicable section of the Internal Revenue Code.

# ᄅᄅ Liability for Nonmanagement

Trustees are policy makers and overseers and must delegate the actual administration of the museum to the staff. Board members cannot, however, delegate their oversight functions; to do so is nonmanagement or dereliction of duty for which trustees can incur liability. A trustee has a duty of active and positive loyalty, which in practice means giving close personal attention to management matters. It is not enough to hire an accounting firm to keep the museum's financial records; the board must monitor the work of that firm. The board retains ultimate responsibility for all activity carried out by both staff and contract personnel.

Although one case of excessive delegation involved the board of a hospital, that decision has implications for all nonprofit organizations. The finance committee of the board seldom if ever met, and the board left the major fiscal and investment decisions to the total discretion of the board's treasurer. Exceptionally high liquid cash reserves were kept in bank accounts that did not accrue interest. Some of these accounts were in banks of which the hospital trustees were officers, although it was not proven that the trustees had knowledge of the deposits. The board was sued for failure to manage and self-dealing. Former patients were allowed to prosecute the litigation for the benefit of the hospital. The court found for the plaintiffs, although the defendant trustees were not required to pay any judgments or the plaintiffs' legal costs, and over the plaintiffs' objection the court allowed the hospital to reimburse the board members for the extensive legal costs each sustained. The court did require the board to revise its fiscal oversight functions and ordered each trustee to make detailed disclosure of personal connections with any entity engaged in financial dealings with the hospital.

# ᄅᄅᄅᄅ Constitutional Liabilities

Liability for actions that violate certain constitutional rights of the individual—usually the right to freedom of speech and association—can be imposed only upon board members of institutions that are part of local, state or federal government. There must be some type of action taken in the name of, or cloaked with, the authority of government to create liability for a board member. Boards appointed to manage government-affiliated museums exercise the authority of the government that appoints them.

The United States Constitution does not provide direct protection against action taken by individuals, boards or institutions not somehow affiliated with government. The courts are mindful of the stark contrast between the constitutional rights afforded those employed or affected by the actions of governmental organizations and the absence of constitutional protections against the same actions by private persons or entities. In view of this duality of treatment, judges may attempt to find the requisite governmental presence where the deprivation of a fundamental constitutional right has been alleged. Trustees of museums that have government affiliations should be aware of their heightened vulnerability to a suit of this nature. The immunity from suit and liability normally enjoyed by the government official is limited when constitutional wrongs, or torts, are alleged, although when museum trustees who are also government officials are sued they may be provided legal services by the affiliated government.

The concept of constitutional wrong became a monetary reality for trustees of a community college. Acting on the college president's recommendation, the board voted to terminate a faculty member. The instructor, who taught journalism and acted as adviser to the school newspaper, was accused of causing the paper to print information alleging that the chairman of the board improperly influenced the college administration to award an equipment contract to a firm managed by the chairman's nephew. The chairman of the board was also an officer of the equipment firm. At the conclusion of the trial the judge ordered the college to reinstate the faculty member and entered judgment against the college president and the trustees who voted for dismissal to pay more than $10,000 each for violating the faculty member's right to freedom of speech. The judge also assessed the plaintiff's legal fees and costs individually against the board members and the college president. The chairman of the board escaped liability because he did not attend the board meeting at which the termination action was taken. A trustee who dissented from the vote to terminate the instructor also escaped liability. The appeals court agreed in principle with the trial court, although it absolved the trustees of personal monetary liability except for a total of $2,500 to be paid by them as a group or jointly. The college president was required to pay an additional $2,500 because of his actions.

# ⌐⌐⌐⌐ Liabilities of Pension Fund Trustees

The trustees of a museum's pension fund assume a specific category of liabilities. The Employee Retirement Income Security Act of 1974 (ERISA) looks to the fiduciary standards of the common law trustee as the measure for accountability and liability of trustees of employee pension funds. That fiduciary standard, in combination with the act's other complex regulations and reporting requirements, has caused many museums to transfer their pension plans to larger units either privately or governmentally operated. To minimize the possibility of technical or other breaches of duty, those museums continuing to administer private pension plans should seek the advice of counsel experienced in pension law. The board of a museum with a separate plan should also ascertain that all trustees for the pension fund are protected by insurance providing the broadest possible coverage. A special policy may be necessary for trustees with pension fund responsibilities, as they are frequently excluded from insurance policies covering board members acting in their regular capacities.

# ⌐⌐⌐⌐⌐⌐⌐ Indemnification and Insurance Protection

If the museum has the financial capacity, it can provide legal defense costs and indemnify or reimburse board members for most expenses and liabilities deriving from board service. The particulars of the protection available from the museum may depend on applicable state law and the provisions in its bylaws or articles of incorporation that authorize indemnification of trustees for expenses and liabilities related to board service.

Each museum board should adopt a bylaw or include in its articles of incorporation authorization for the institution to defend its members or pay trustees for extraordinary expenses attendant upon board service. These provisions should extend board authority to indemnify as far as the law permits, reserving to the board discretion to refuse to provide defense costs or to indemnify from the organization's treasury for selected settlements or adverse judgments. The facts of any given situation will vary, and a trustee probably will not be indemnified if he is adjudged to have acted willfully or with gross negligence. In such cases the trustee often is precluded from indemnification by applicable law or a specific ruling of the court.

Insurance can be another bulwark for trustees, providing far broader protection than is available under the rules for indemnification. Museum boards should consider purchase by the institution of a policy specifically designed to give maximum protection to board members and officers. Such protection is the norm for the business world, and boards will find many of their best candidates refusing to join unless insurance is in force. Insurance should also be obtained to cover the museum director and other senior staff who work with the board as well as nontrustees who sit on committees or otherwise assist the board.

The broader insurance policies for trustees and officers provide for defense costs and indemnification for nearly all liabilities relating to board service, except for dishonest conduct or that intentionally pursued by a board member from which he secures personal gain. Protection for libelous statements by board members typically is not provided in such policies, although protection for libel suits against trustees can usually be included in the museum's general liability insurance policy. Pension fund trustees may be excluded from the trustees' and officers' policy unless they are specially provided for and additional premiums are paid. There may be other situations in which an insurance company would refuse to pay, arguing that the activities were contrary to public policy and, as a deterrent to others, the trustee should be forced to pay. If a trustee or officer purposely attempted to deprive an individual of recognized constitutional rights, a court might decide the insurance company need not reimburse defense or other legal costs or pay an adverse judgment.

The cost to a museum of insurance to protect its board members from potential liabilities related to their service is small by comparison to value received. Insurance enables board members to act affirmatively, secure in the knowledge that they will not be monetarily liable for any actions performed in good faith and that the museum esteems their service and stands behind them.

For most institutions the premium cost for this coverage is a few thousand dollars a year, varying upon dollar limits of coverage, the amount of the deductible and the percentage of coinsurance. The extent of a museum's activities and size of its board are other underwriting factors. Premiums will be higher if protection for pension trustees or libel suits is included. Even though it appears a claim will not exceed the amount of the deductible, the insurance carrier must be notified whenever a matter arises that might escalate into a claim under the policy.

Coinsurance is that percentage of any loss to be paid by the museum; 5 percent is typical. Insurers frequently insist upon coinsurance to encourage better board management and discourage trustee claims under a policy.

The circumstances surrounding each claim are carefully investigated by the insurance company. If negligence on the part of trustees is found, the premium will be increased. In extreme cases insurance for the board will be canceled. If one company has determined the museum board to be a poor insurance risk, coverage will be difficult to procure from others underwriting this type of policy.

In closing it should be emphasized again that with careful management of those aspects of service demanding attention, the probability of being held to account is remote. It is important that trustees be aware of these circumstances, however, and that they be fully conversant with the legal status they assume in joining a museum's governing board. This awareness need not be inhibiting; indeed, it should enhance trustees' effectiveness. With full knowledge of its legal and ethical obligations, museum trusteeship can achieve its potential as a rich and rewarding experience of service.

# Further Readings

References are listed alphabetically by chapter and section. Occasional annotations describe briefly the importance of the source or further identify the discussion in the text that it is meant to amplify. Related topics are discussed at various places throughout the text. Since not all bibliographic citations are cross-referenced, the reader searching for sources on a particular topic should consult the index and the citations listed for each discussion recorded there.

## General

### BIBLIOGRAPHIES

The sections on museum management and museum trusteeship in the following bibliographies will point museum trustees to many useful sources.

Benedict, Stephen, and Coe, Linda C. *Arts Management: An Annotated Bibliography*. Rev. ed. New York: Center for Arts Information, 1980.

Gorr, Louis F., ed. "A Museum Management Bibliography." *Museum News* 58 (May/June 1980): 71–84, and (July/August 1980): 67–77.

Rath, Frederick L., Jr., and O'Connell, Merrilyn Rogers, eds. *A Bibliography on Historical Organization Practices: Administration*. Nashville: AASLH, 1980.

### COLLECTIONS OF ESSAYS

The following collections contain numerous essays of interest to museum trustees. Citations to them in this bibliography will be in brief form, including only author and/or title, and editors' names.

Connors, Tracy Daniel, ed. *The Nonprofit Organization Handbook*. New York: McGraw-Hill, 1980.

Ingram, Richard T., and Associates. *Handbook of College and University Trusteeship*. San Francisco: Jossey-Bass, 1980.

Zaltman, Gerald, ed. *Management Principles for Nonprofit Agencies and Organizations*. New York: AMACOM, 1979.

## Chapter I. Introduction to Trusteeship

Alexander, Edward P. *Museums in Motion*. Nashville: AASLH, 1979.

Blaine, John. "Accountability to the Hand That Feeds You." *Museum News* 57 (May/June 1979): 34–36. Focuses on the government-supported museum.

Kimche, Lee. "American Museums: The Vital Statistics." *Museum News* 59 (October 1980): 53–57.

Meyer, Karl E. *The Art Museum: Power, Money, Ethics*. New York: William Morrow, 1979. A critique of art museums and their management, including trustees.

Weil, Stephen E. "Vincible Ignorance: Museums and the Law." *Museum News* 59 (September/October 1979): 31–36.

# MUSEUMS

American Association for State and Local History. *Directory of Historical Societies and Agencies in the United States and Canada.* 12th ed. Nashville: AASLH, 1981.

American Association of Museums. *The Official Museum Directory, 1981.* Skokie, Ill.: AAM and National Register Publishing Co., 1980. Basic information on 5,500 museums and related institutions in the United States and Canada.

Burcaw, G. Ellis. *Introduction to Museum Work.* Nashville: AASLH, 1975.

*People ex rel. Scott v. George F. Harding Museum,* 58 Ill. App. 3d 408, 374 N.E.2d 756, 761 (1978). The court determined that a museum is a charitable organization.

Schlebecker, John, and Peterson, Gale E. *Living Historical Farms Handbook.* Washington, D.C.: Smithsonian Institution, 1972.

Swinney, H. J., ed. *Professional Standards for Museum Accreditation.* Washington, D.C.: AAM, 1978.

# TRUSTEES

Cunningham, Robert M., Jr. *Governing Hospitals: Trustees and the New Accountabilities.* Chicago: American Hospital Association, 1976.

*Donahue v. Rodd Electrotype Company of New England, Inc.,* 367 Mass. 578, 328 N.E.2d 505 (1975). Corporate directors were held to a good faith and inherent fairness standard of conduct.

Greenleaf, Robert K. *Trustees as Servants.* Cambridge, Mass.: Center for Applied Studies, 1975.

Loring, Augustus P. *A Trustee's Handbook.* 6th ed. Revision by James F. Farr. Boston: Little, Brown & Co., 1962.

Naumer, Helmuth J. *Of Mutual Respect and Other Things: An Essay on Museum Trusteeship.* Washington, D.C.: AAM, 1977.

Scott, Austin W. "The Fiduciary Principle." *California Law Review* 37 (December 1949): 539–55.

————. "The Trustee's Duty of Loyalty." *Harvard Law Review* 49 (February 1936): 521–65.

# HISTORICAL PRECEDENTS

American Bar Association, Committee on Corporate Laws, Section of Corporation, Banking, and Business Law. *Model Nonprofit Corporation Act.* Philadelphia: ALI-ABA Committee on Continuing Professional Education, 1964.

*Beard v. Achenbach Memorial Hospital Association,* 170 F.2d 859 (10th Cir. 1948); *Ray v. Homewood Hospital, Inc.,* 223 Minn. 440, 27 N.W.2d 409, 411 (1947). The courts applied the corporate standard to charitable trusts and corporations.

Berle, Adolph A., Jr. "Corporate Powers as Powers in Trust." *Harvard Law Review* 44 (May 1931): 1049–74.

Boylan, William A. "Endowment Funds: Collision of Corporate and Trust Standards." *Business Lawyer* 18 (April 1963): 807–18.

"California Nonprofit Corporation Law: A Symposium." *University of San Francisco Law Review* 13 (Summer 1979): 729–912.

Chidlaw, Ben E. "Non-Profit and Charitable Corporations in Colorado." *University of Colorado Law Review* 36 (Fall 1963): 9–35.

*Commonwealth v. Barnes Foundation,* 398 Pa. 458, 159 A.2d 500 (1960). Finding that a foundation owes a duty to the public, the court required the foundation to open its works of art to at least restricted public viewing as a condition for its tax exemption. The cultural value of a museum's assets was also established.

"Corporations—Fiduciary Duty: Fiduciary Duty of a Director of a Nonprofit Corporation under D.C. Nonprofit Corporation Act Is Similar to Duty Imposed upon a Director of a Business Corporation." *Catholic University Law Review* 24 (Spring 1975): 657–66.

Ellman, I. M. "On Developing a Law of Nonprofit Corporations." *Arizona State Law Journal* (Summer 1979): 153–64.

"The Enforcement of Charitable Trusts in America: A History of Evolving Social Attitudes." *Virginia Law Review* 54 (April 1968): 436–65.

"The Fiduciary Duties of Loyalty and Care Associated with the Directors and Trustees of Charitable Organizations." *Virginia Law Review* 64 (April 1978): 449–65. Argues for a modified corporate standard to be applied to both charitable corporations and charitable trusts.

Fisch, Edith L.; Freed, Doris Jonas; and Schachter, Esther R. *Charities and Charitable Foundations*. Pomona, N.Y.: Lond Publications, 1974.

Fremont-Smith, Marion R. "Duties and Powers of Charitable Fiduciaries: The Law of Trusts and the Correction of Abuses." *UCLA Law Review* 13 (May 1966): 1041–59.

―――. *Foundations and Government*. New York: Russell Sage Foundation, 1965. Early chapters review the development of the charitable trust and the nonprofit corporation.

Fryer, William T., III, and Hoaglund, David R. "New California Nonprofit Corporation Law: A Unique Approach." *Pepperdine Law Review* 7 (Fall 1979): 1–40.

*Graham Bros. Co. v. Galloway Woman's College*, 190 Ark. 692, 81 S.W.2d 837, 840 (1935). The court applied a modified trust standard.

Haller, Louis P. "The Model Non-Profit Corporation Act." *Baylor Law Review* 9 (Summer 1957): 309–21. Pages 312–17 give a historical sketch of early colonial and state laws that allowed the incorporation of nonprofit organizations.

Hamilton, Denis. "The Trustee and the National Museums." *Museums Journal* 77 (December 1977): 119–20.

Hands, Arthur R. *Charities and Social Aid in Greece and Rome*. London: Thames and Hudson, 1968.

Hansmann, Henry B. "The Role of Nonprofit Enterprise." *Yale Law Journal* 89 (April 1980): 835–901.

*Jackson v. Statler Foundation*, 496 F.2d 623 (2d Cir. 1974). The legislative history of the charitable exemption section of the Internal Revenue Code was reviewed.

Jones, Gareth. *History of the Law of Charity, 1532–1827*. Cambridge: At the University Press, 1969.

Kocourek, Albert, and Wigmore, John H. *Evolution of Law: Select Readings on the Origin and Development of Legal Institutions*. Vol. 1: *Sources of Ancient and Primitive Law*; Vol. 2: *Primitive and Ancient Legal Institutions*. Boston: Little, Brown & Co., 1915.

Mace, Myles L. "Standards of Care for Trustees." *Harvard Business Review* 54 (January/February 1976): 14 ff.

*Manlove v. Wilmington General Hospital*, 53 Del. 338, 169 A.2d 18, 22 (Super. Ct.), Aff'd., 54 Del. 15, 174 A.2d 135 (1961). Charitable corporations were characterized as quasi-public institutions.

Marsh, Gordon H. "Governance of Non-Profit Organizations: An Appropriate Standard of Conduct for Trustees and Directors of Museums and Other Cultural Institutions." *Dickinson Law Review* 85 (Summer 1981): 101–21.

Middleditch, Leigh B., Jr. "Navigating for the Fiduciary Who Ships Out with the Not-For-Profit." *Ninth Annual Institute on Estate Planning, University of Miami Law Center*, chap. 9. New York: Matthew Bender, 1975.

Oleck, Howard L. *Non-Profit Corporations, Organizations, and Associations*. 4th ed. Englewood Cliffs, N.J.: Prentice-Hall, 1980. Section 215 treats the fiduciary status of directors.

*People v. Larkin*, 413 F. Supp. 978 (N.D. Cal. 1976); *Holt v. College of Osteopathic Physicians and Surgeons*, 61 Cal. 2d 750, 394 P.2d 932, 40 Cal. Rptr. 244 (1964). The courts applied the trust standard of loyalty and care to charitable trusts and corporations.

"Report of the Committee on Charitable Trusts: Duties of Charitable Trust Trustees and Charitable Corporation Directors." *Real Property, Probate, and Trust Journal* 2 (Winter 1967): 545–64.

Restatement (Second) of Trusts, section 379, comment b (1959). A board of directors acts in a fiduciary capacity to the charitable corporation.

Rickett, C.E.F. "Charitable Giving in English and Roman Law: A Comparison of Method." *Cambridge Law Journal* 38 (April 1979): 118–47.

Sherman, Charles Phineas. *Roman Law in the Modern World*. Vol. 1: *History of Roman Law and Its Descent into English, French, German, Italian, Spanish, and Other Modern Law*. Boston: Boston Book Company, 1917.

Smieton, Mary. "The Trustee and the National Museums." *Museums Journal* 77 (December 1977): 117–18.

*Stern v. Lucy Webb Hayes National Training School for Deaconesses and Missionaries*, 381 F. Supp. 1003 (D.D.C. 1974). Commonly known as the Sibley Hospital case. The fiduciary duties of common law trustees were compared with the fiduciary duties of corporate directors.

# Chapter II. Responsibilities of Museum Trustees

## GENERAL POLICY MAKING

American Association of Museums, Committee on Ethics. *Museum Ethics*. Washington, D.C.: AAM, 1978. Pages 27–28 discuss museum governance.

Association of Art Museum Directors. *Professional Practices in Art Museums*. Rev. ed. Savannah, Ga.: AAMD, 1981.

Burns, William A. "Trustees: Duties and Responsibilities." *Museum News* 41 (December 1962): 22–23.

Copeland, Mrs. Lammot du Pont. *The Role of Trustees: Selection and Responsibilities*. Nashville: AASLH Technical Leaflet 72. From *History News* 29 (March 1974).

Milrad, Aaron, and Agnew, Ella. *The Art World: Law, Business, & Practice in Canada*. Toronto: Merritt Publishing Co., 1980. See pages 90–100.

Swartchild, William G., Jr. "How Shared Policy Making Can Work." *Museum News* 59 (May/June 1981): 56 ff.

## POLICY AND ADMINISTRATION

Conrad, William R., and Glenn, William E. *The Effective Volunteer Board of Directors*. Chicago: Swallow Press, 1976. Chapter 4 analyzes the "delicate balance" between trustees and professional staff.

Nason, John W. "Responsibilities of the Governing Board." In Ingram, op. cit., chap. 3. Focuses on the trustee's role as overseer, as contrasted to the administrative responsibilities of the chief executive.

Young, Donald R., and Moore, Wilbert E. *Trusteeship and the Management of Foundations*. New York: Russell Sage Foundation, 1969. Pages 15–23 outline the principles of lay control of salaried professionals.

Young, Virginia G. *The Library Trustee: A Practical Guidebook*. New York: R. R. Bowker, 1969. Contains essays on the range of trustee responsibilities.

## POLICY STATEMENTS

Begemann, Egbert H. "The Price Is Never Right." *Museum News* 51 (May 1973): 32–35. Argues against museums' disposing of works of art, especially to private collectors.

Connors, Tracy D. "The Board of Directors." In Connors, op. cit., sec. 2, chap. 4. Discusses the basic responsibilities of boards of trustees.

Corson, John J. "Participating in Policy Making and Management." In Ingram, op. cit., chap. 7.

Fisch, Edith L.; Freed, Doris Jonas; and Schachter, Esther R. *Charities and Charitable Foundations*. Pomona, N.Y.: Lond Publications, 1974. Section 663 deals with the disposition of property upon termination of a charitable corporation.

Greenleaf, Robert K. *Trustees as Servants*. Cambridge, Mass.: Center for Applied Studies, 1975.

Hopkins, Bruce R. *The Law of Tax-Exempt Organizations*. 3d ed. New York: John Wiley & Sons, 1979. Chapter 5 deals with organizational and operational tests of charitable organizations.

Oleck, Howard L. *Non-Profit Corporations, Organizations, and Associations*. 4th ed. Englewood Cliffs, N.J.: Prentice-Hall, 1980. Chapter 42 deals with the effects of dissolution and transfer of property.

Practising Law Institute. *Non-Profit Cultural Organizations*. New York: PLI, 1979. Chapter 1 deals with structuring tax-exempt nonprofit cultural organizations.

Treusch, Paul E., and Sugarman, Norman A. *Tax-Exempt Charitable Organizations*. Philadelphia: ALI-ABA Committee on Continuing Professional Education, 1979.

## SPECIFIC POLICY MAKING

### LONG-RANGE PLANNING

Alexander, John O. "Planning and Management in Nonprofit Organizations." In Connors, op. cit., sec. 2, chap. 3.

Dorsey, Rhoda M. "Engaging in Institutional Planning." In Ingram, op. cit., chap. 9.

Edwards, Charles A. "Development in Context." *Museum News* 56 (May/June 1978): 40–43.

Ela, Patrick. "One Museum's Planning Experience." *Museum News* 58 (July/August 1980): 33–37.

Hendon, William S. *Analyzing an Art Museum*. New York: Praeger Publishers, 1979. Presents a cost-benefit analysis of an art museum and its activities.

Hennessey, Paul, and Associates. *Managing Nonprofit Agencies for Results: A Systems Approach to Long-Range Planning*. San Francisco: Public Management Institute, 1978.

King, William R. "Strategic Planning in Nonprofit Organizations." In Zaltman, op. cit., chap. 9.

McHugh, Alice. "Strategic Planning for Museums." *Museum News* 58 (July/August 1980): 23–29.

Sherrell, Cindy. *Thoughts on Museum Planning*. 2d ed. Austin: Texas Historical Commission Department of Museum Services, 1978.

### ATTENTION TO THE TAX EXEMPTION

Conable, Barber. "Tax Impact on Charitable Organizations." *Catholic Lawyer* 24 (Summer 1979): 251–57.

Fisch, Edith L.; Freed, Doris Jonas; and Schachter, Esther R. *Charities and Charitable Foundations*. Pomona, N.Y.: Lond Publications, 1974. Title 5 deals with the tax treatment afforded charitable organizations.

Hopkins, Bruce R. *The Law of Tax-Exempt Organizations*. 3d ed. New York: John Wiley & Sons, 1979. Chapter 38 deals with the maintenance of tax-exempt status.

Lane, Marc J. *Legal Handbook for Nonprofit Organizations*. New York: AMACOM, 1980. Chapters 6, 7 and 8 discuss federal income tax exemption, unrelated business taxable income and benefits such as exemption from state sales taxes and special postage rates.

Liles, Kenneth H., and Roth, Stephen E. "The Unrelated Business Income Problems of Art Museums." *Connecticut Law Review* 10 (Spring 1978): 638–52.

Montgomery, Alan L. "Lobbying by Public Charities under the Tax Reform Act of 1976: The New Elective Provisions of Section 501(h)—Safe Harbor or Trap for the Unwary?" *Taxes* 56 (August 1978): 449–61.

"Museums Find a New Patron: The Retail Market." *Business Week*, October 24, 1977, pp. 135–36; also published in *Marketing in Nonprofit Organizations*, edited by Patrick J. Montana, pp. 281–84. New York: AMACOM, 1978.

Nix, James H. "Limitations on the Lobbying of Section 501(c) (3) Organizations: A Choice for the Public Charities." *West Virginia Law Review* 81 (Spring 1979): 407–26.

Oleck, Howard L. *Non-Profit Corporations, Organizations, and Associations*. 4th ed. Englewood Cliffs, N.J.: Prentice-Hall, 1980. Chapters 30 and 31 deal with state taxes and exemptions.

Practising Law Institute. *Non-Profit Cultural Organizations*. New York: PLI, 1979. Chapter 8 deals with unrelated business taxable income of nonprofit organizations.

"Profitable Related Business Activities and Charitable Exemption under Section 501 (c) (3)." *George Washington University Law Review* 44 (January 1976): 270–86.

Treusch, Paul E., and Sugarman, Norman A. *Tax-Exempt Charitable Organizations*. Philadelphia: ALI-ABA Committee on Continuing Professional Education, 1979. Chapter 6 deals with tax on unrelated business income.

Washburn, Barbara J. "New Tax Act Defines 'Substantial' Lobbying—But Charities Must Elect To Be Covered." *Taxes* 55 (May 1977): 291–99.

Weithorn, Stanley S. "Practitioner's Planning Guide to the New Lobbying Rules for Public Charities." *Journal of Taxation* 46 (May 1977): 294–99.

## COMPLIANCE WITH REGULATORY LAWS

*Alperin v. United States*, U.S. District Court for the Western District of Tennessee, No. C–71–482 (December 2, 1971). The chairman of the board of a nonprofit theater was found personally liable for $16,000 plus interest and penalties because of theater's failure to pay over employee income taxes withheld, according to Internal Revenue Code, sections 6671 and 6672. Judgment was satisfied upon payment of $10,000 to the Internal Revenue Service.

Fisch, Edith L.; Freed, Doris Jonas; and Schachter, Esther R. *Charities and Charitable Foundations*. Pomona, N.Y.: Lond Publications, 1974. Title 4 deals with government regulation of charitable organizations.

Larson, Arthur. *The Law of Workmen's Compensation*. New York: Matthew Bender, 1979. Sections 50.40–44 deal with the effect of workmen's compensation laws on nonprofit organizations.

*Piascik v. Cleveland Museum of Art*, 426 F. Supp. 779 (N.D. Ohio 1976). The court determined that an art museum receiving federal assistance for education programs must comply with federal laws prohibiting sex discrimination, and persons alleging discrimination can sue the museum directly.

United States Code, Title 26, section 3121(k). States the requirements for an election by an organization and its employees concerning whether to be part of the social security system.

Weil, Stephen E. "Vincible Ignorance: Museums and the Law." *Museum News* 59 (September/October 1979): 31–36. Discusses some of the regulatory requirements imposed on museums.

## COLLECTIONS MANAGEMENT

Association of Art Museum Directors. *Professional Practices in Art Museums.* Rev. ed. Savannah, Ga.: AAMD, 1981.

Dudley, Dorothy H.; Wilkinson, Irma Bezold; and Others. *Museum Registration Methods.* 3d ed. Washington, D.C.: AAM, 1979. This basic text on museum registration treats all aspects of collections management.

Lewis, Ralph H. *Manual for Museums.* Washington, D.C.: Department of the Interior, 1976. Discusses all aspects of collections management.

Malaro, Marie C. "Collections Management Policies." *Museum News* 58 (November/December 1979): 57–61.

————. "A Lawyer Advises on Collections Policy." *History News* 35 (October 1980): 13–14.

Neal, Arminta; Haglund, Kristine; and Webb, Elizabeth. "Evolving a Policy Manual." *Museum News* 56 (January/February 1978): 26–30.

### Acquisitions

DuBoff, Leonard D. *The Deskbook of Art Law.* Washington, D.C.: Federal Publications, 1977. See pages 913–24.

Feldman, Franklin, and Weil, Stephen E. *Art Works: Law, Policy, Practice.* New York: Practising Law Institute, 1974. See pages 1093–1111.

### Conservation

Keck, Caroline K. "Conservation's Cloudy Future." *Museum News* 58 (May/June 1980): 35–39.

National Conservation Advisory Council. *Conservation of Cultural Property in the United States.* Washington, D.C.: NCAC, Smithsonian Institution, 1976.

Swinney, H. J., ed. *Professional Standards for Museum Accreditation.* Washington, D.C.: AAM, 1978. Pages 49–50 treat conservation and preservation questions for on-site evaluations.

### Insurance

*Harris v. Attorney General,* 31 Conn. Supp. 93, 324 A.2d 279, 286–87 (1974). Although Restatement (Second) of Trusts, section 176, comment b (1959), states that the duty of trustees in preserving assets and in acquiring insurance is "to take reasonable steps to procure such insurance as is customarily taken by prudent men," the trustees of a museum were found not to have a duty to insure its collections. The court determined that the practice of museums at that time was to insure their collections for a nominal amount or for nothing at all because art treasures are irreplaceable.

Nauert, Patricia, and Block, Caroline M. *Fine Arts Insurance: A Handbook for Art Museums.* Santa Barbara, Cal.: AAMD, 1979.

Shirey, David. "Insuring Art." *Art News* 74 (February 1975): 57–59.

Tillotson, Robert G. *Museum Security.* Edited by Diana D. Menkes. Paris: International Council of Museums, 1977.

### Deaccessioning

"Acquisition or Inquisition?" *Museum News* 51 (May 1973): entire issue.

DuBoff, Leonard D. *The Deskbook of Art Law.* Washington, D.C.: Federal Publications, 1977. See pages 933–44.

Feldman, Franklin, and Weil, Stephen E. *Art Works: Law, Policy, Practice.* New York: Practising Law Institute, 1974. See pages 1113–34.

McQuade, Walter. "Norton Simon's Great Museum Caper." *Fortune* 102 (August 25, 1980): 78–84.

*Matter of Horticultural Society of New York, Inc.* (Supreme Court, New York County, 1980). Reported in *New York Law Journal*, April 1, 1980. The court approved the trustees' determination to sell and the mode of sale of collection objects.

Merryman, John Henry, and Elsen, Albert E. *Law, Ethics and the Visual Arts.* New York: Matthew Bender, 1979. See section 7, pages 107–67.

## THE PHYSICAL PLANT

*Harris v. Attorney General,* 31 Conn. Supp. 93, 324 A.2d 279, 287 (1974). The court determined that museum trustees have a duty, in providing security for the collection, "to exercise that care and prudence which an ordinarily prudent person would who was entrusted with the management of like property for another."

Nelson, Charles A. "Managing Resources." In Ingram, op. cit., chap. 16.

Vance, David. "Planning Ahead: The Registrar's Role in a Building Program." In *Museum Registration Methods* by Dorothy H. Dudley, Irma Bezold Wilkinson, and Others, pp. 395–408. 3d ed. Washington, D.C.: AAM, 1979. Discusses the principles for design of facilities for collections.

## USE OF THE COLLECTIONS AND RELATED ACTIVITIES

Black, Craig C. "The Case for Research." *Museum News* 58 (May/June 1980): 51–53.

———. "New Strains on Our Resources." *Museum News* 56 (January/February 1978): 18–22.

*Commonwealth v. Barnes Foundation,* 398 Pa. 458, 159 A.2d 500 (1960). The court determined that a foundation is required to open its works of art to public viewing.

Ludwig, John. "The Role of the Performing Arts." *Museum News* 45 (January 1967): 40–41.

Newsom, Barbara Y. "A Decade of Uncertainty for Museum Educators." *Museum News* 58 (May/June 1980): 46–50.

Richoux, Jeanette; Serota-Braden, Jill; and Demyttenaere, Nancy. "A Policy for Collections Access." *Museum News* 59 (July/August 1981): 43–47.

## FINANCIAL RESPONSIBILITIES

Daughtrey, William H., Jr., and Gross, Malvern J., Jr. *Museum Accounting Handbook.* Washington, D.C.: AAM, 1978. Contains basic accounting information useful for carrying out trustees' financial responsibilities.

Kobrin, Lawrence A. "A Practical Guide to Counseling Volunteers." *Practical Lawyer* 25 (July 1979): 29–42. Contains information on many aspects of trustees' financial responsibilities.

## PLANNING AND BUDGETING

Birnberg, Jacob. "Accounting Information for Operating Decisions." In Zaltman, op. cit., chap. 13.

Leduc, Robert. "Financial Management and Budgeting." In Connors, op. cit., sec. 6, chap. 2.

Nelson, Charles A., and Turk, Fredrick J. *Financial Management for the Arts*. New York: Associated Councils of the Arts, 1975.

## FUND RAISING

Buhler, Leslie. "The Business of Membership." *Museum News* 59 (November/December 1980): 42–49.

Coe, Linda C.; Denney, Rebecca; and Rogers, Anne. *Cultural Directory II: Federal Funding and Services for the Arts and Humanities*. Washington, D.C.: Smithsonian Institution, 1980.

Commission on Private Philanthropy and Public Needs. John H. Filer, Chairman. *Giving in America*. Washington, D.C.: Commission on Private Philanthropy and Public Needs, 1975.

Hoffman, Marilyn. "Writing Realistic Grant Proposals." *Museum News* 58 (January/February 1980): 48–53.

Kurzig, Carol M. *Foundation Fundamentals: A Guide for Grantseekers*. New York: Foundation Center, 1980.

Radock, Michael, and Jacobson, Harvey K. "Securing Resources." In Ingram, op. cit., chap. 14.

"Sources of Revenue for the Nonprofit Organization." In Connors, op. cit., sec. 4.

Steinbach, Alice, and Selph, Mark D. "Bond Issue Politics." *Museum News* 57 (May/June 1979): 37–42.

Teitell, Conrad. "Introduction to Charitable Giving: Charitable Remainder Unitrusts and Charitable Remainder Annuity Trusts." In *Institute on Charitable Giving*, pp. 335–423. Notre Dame, Ind.: Notre Dame University Law School, 1976.

White, Virginia P. *Grants: How To Find Out about Them and What To Do Next*. New York: Plenum Press, 1975.

———. *Grants for the Arts*. New York: Plenum Press, 1980.

## INVESTMENT AND CASH MANAGEMENT

*Blankenship v. Boyle*, 329 F. Supp. 1089 (D.D.C. 1971), Aff'd., 511 F.2d 447 (D.C. Cir. 1975). The court determined that a basic duty of trustees is to invest trust funds so they will be productive of income. The court also found that the trustees engaged in self-dealing by using trust assets so as to benefit other entities with which they were connected, even though they may not have profited personally.

Bogert, G. G., and Bogert, G. T. *Trusts and Trustees*. 2d ed., rev. St. Paul, Minn.: West Publishing Co., 1977. Sections 431–42 deal with the cy pres doctrine.

Cary, William L., and Bright, C. *The Developing Law of Endowment Funds: "The Law and the Lore" Revisited*. New York: Ford Foundation, 1974. Pages 48–50 deal with the delegation of investment decisions.

Committee on Charitable Trusts and Foundations. "Delegation of Investment Responsibility by Trustees of Charitable Trusts and Corporations." *Real Property, Probate, and Trust Journal* 9 (Winter 1974): 583–95.

Fisch, Edith L. "Changing Concepts and Cy Pres." *Cornell Law Quarterly* 44 (Spring 1959): 382–93.

Gettleman, R. W., and Hodgman, D. R. "Judicial Construction of Charitable Bequests: Theory vs. Practice." *Chicago-Kent Law Review* 53 (1977): 659–69.

Herzlinger, Regina E., and Sherman, H. David. "Advantages of Fund Accounting in Nonprofits." *Harvard Business Review* 58 (May/June 1980): 94–105.

Kolb, Charles E. M. "Delegation of Authority to Committees of the Board of Directors: Director's Liabilities." *University of Baltimore Law Review* 9 (Winter 1980): 189–216.

Kutner, Luis. *Legal Aspects of Charitable Trusts and Foundations.* New York: Commerce Clearing House, 1970. Pages 230–48 deal with trust investment policies.

*Lynch v. John M. Redfield Foundation,* 9 Cal. App. 3d 293, 88 Cal. Rptr. 86, 51 A.L.R.3d 1284 (1970). The court determined that the duty of a trustee is to make trust funds productive.

Oleck, Howard L. *Non-Profit Corporations, Organizations, and Associations.* 4th ed. Englewood Cliffs, N.J.: Prentice-Hall, 1980. Chapter 26 deals with the functions of committees.

Pocock, John W. "Reporting Finances." In Ingram, op. cit., chap. 15.

Scott, Austin W. *The Law of Trusts.* 3d ed. Boston: Little, Brown & Co., 1967. Sections 395–401 deal with the doctrine of cy pres.

*Stern v. Lucy Webb Hayes National Training School for Deaconesses and Missionaries,* 381 F. Supp. 1003 (D.D.C. 1974). The court determined that it is a breach of fiduciary duty for trustees to keep excessive amounts of cash in non-interest-bearing bank accounts, or, without fully disclosing to the board the circumstances of their personal financial interests, to transact business with the organization.

Welles, Chris. "Nonprofit Institutions." In *Abuse on Wall Street: Conflicts of Interest in the Securities Markets,* edited by Roy Schotland, pp. 498–564. Westport, Conn.: Quorum Books, for the Twentieth Century Fund, 1980. Pages 515–32 deal with the problems created by trustees who handle or control their organization's investments.

## ACCOUNTING AND AUDIT

Choka, Allen D. "The New Role of the Audit Committee." *Practical Lawyer* 23 (September 1977): 53–60.

Clapp, Jane. *Professional Ethics and Insignia.* Metuchen, N.J.: Scarecrow Press, 1974. Pages 9–10 contain the accountants' code of ethics, which states that "independence" is impaired if the accountant or auditor is connected to the enterprise in the capacity of officer or employee.

Leduc, Robert, and Callaghan, Christopher T. "Bookkeeping Procedures for the Nonprofit Organization." In Connors, op. cit., sec. 6, chap. 4.

Loo, Thomas S., and Feller, Lloyd H. "The Audit Committee." In *Ninth Annual Institute on Securities Regulation.* New York: PLI, 1978.

Racek, Timothy J. "Nonprofit Accounting and Financial Reporting." In Connors, op. cit., sec. 6, chap. 1.

## FINANCIAL SUPPORT FOR THE GOVERNMENT MUSEUM

Corrick, George W., and Detweiler, John S. "Involving Community Leadership and Citizens." In Connors, op. cit., sec. 5, chap. 3.

Daly, John Jay. "How To Tell Your Story to a Legislative Body." In Connors, op. cit., sec. 5, chap. 8.

Gasser, James. "Why Cities Need Museums." *Museum News* 57 (May/June 1979): 26–28.

Montana, Patrick J., ed. *Marketing in Nonprofit Organizations.* New York: AMACOM, 1978.

## THE BOARD AND THE STAFF

### THE DIRECTOR

Nason, John W. "Responsibilities of the Governing Board." In Ingram, op. cit., chap. 3.

### PERSONNEL POLICIES

Craft, James A. "Managing Human Resources." In Zaltman, op. cit., chap. 3.

"The Grantsmanship Center Personnel Policies." *Grantsmanship Center News* 5 (March/April 1979): 83–87.

Jensen, Jerry. "Personnel Policies for Your Agency: Get Them in Writing Now." *Grantsmanship Center News* 5 (March/April 1979): 17–22, 83.

Lee, Robert D., Jr. *Public Personnel Systems*. Baltimore: University Park Press, 1979.

Mariner, Dorothy A. "Professionalizing the Museum Worker." *Museum News* 50 (June 1972): 14–20.

Miller, Ronald L. *Personnel Policies for Museums: A Handbook for Management*. Washington, D.C.: AAM, 1980.

Practising Law Institute. *Basic Labor Relations, 1979*. New York: PLI, 1979. Chapter 15 deals with the legal considerations in reviewing personnel handbooks.

Richards, Audrey. *Managing Volunteers for Results*. San Francisco: Institute for Fund Raising, 1978.

Straus, Ellen S. "Volunteer Professionalism." *Museum News* 56 (September/October 1977): 24–26.

### Legal Rights

See also the references cited for chapter V, section on Constitutional Liabilities.

*Banyard v. N.L.R.B.*, 505 F.2d 342 (D.C. Cir. 1974). The court held that employees who refuse to violate a state law are protected from dismissal.

Feinman, Jay M. "The Development of the Employment at Will Rule." *American Journal of Legal History* 20 (1976): 118–35.

"Labor Law—1974 Amendments to Labor Management Relations Act—Charitable Institution Exemption Eliminated." *Wayne Law Review* 23 (March 1977): 1143–55.

Practising Law Institute. *Basic Labor Relations, 1977*. New York: PLI, 1977.

———. *Basic Labor Relations, 1979*. New York: PLI, 1979.

*Tameny v. Atlantic Richfield Company*, 27 Cal. 3d 167, 610 P.2d 1330, 164 Cal. Rptr. 839 (1980). The court held that an employee cannot be fired for refusing to violate federal laws.

United States Code, Title 29, section 660(c). The Occupational Safety and Health Act of 1970 prohibits the discharge of an employee for filing complaints, instituting proceedings or testifying in proceedings brought under the act.

Westin, Alan F.; Kurtz, Henry I.; and Robbins, Albert. *Whistle Blowing! Loyalty and Dissent in the Corporation*. New York: McGraw-Hill, 1981. Extensive discussion of legal rights and authorities.

### Grievance Procedures

Lind, Robert C., Jr., and Ullberg, Alan D. "No Fool as a Client." *Museum News* 58 (September/October 1979): 37–42. Describes the steps to take in finding an attorney for specific legal tasks.

Miller, Ronald L. "Grievance Procedures for Non-Union Employees." *Public Personnel Management* 7 (September/October 1978): 302–11.

Nason, John W. "Responsibilities of the Governing Board." In Ingram, op. cit., chap. 3.

## ASSESSING MUSEUM OPERATIONS

Agarwala-Rogers, Rekha, and Alexander, Janet K. "Evaluation of Organizational Activities." In Zaltman, op. cit., chap. 15.

Zwingle, J. L. "Assessing Institutional Performance." In Ingram, op. cit., chap. 20.

## SELF-MANAGEMENT

Paltridge, James Gilbert. "Studying Board Effectiveness." In Ingram, op. cit., chap. 18.

# Chapter III. Structure and Operation of the Board

Conrad, William R., Jr., and Glenn, William E. *The Effective Volunteer Board of Directors: What It Is and How It Works.* Chicago: Swallow Press, 1976. Contains information on board organization and operations.

Freeman, David F. *The Handbook on Private Foundations.* Cabin John, Md.: Seven Locks Press, for the Council on Foundations, 1981. See especially chapter 5, "Governance and Administration."

Ingram, Richard T. "Organizing the Board." In Ingram, op. cit., chap. 5. Contains information on many aspects of board organization, including bylaws, meetings, officers and committees.

Kobrin, Lawrence A. "A Practical Guide to Counseling Volunteers." *Practical Lawyer* 25 (July 1979): 29–42. Contains information on many aspects of the structure and operation of the board.

Lane, Marc J. *Legal Handbook for Nonprofit Organizations.* New York: AMACOM, 1980. Pages 78–88 treat bylaws and records and board committees.

## COMPOSITION OF THE BOARD
## AND SELECTION OF TRUSTEES

See also the references cited for chapter V, section on Selling Products and Services to the Museum.

National Commission on College and University Trustee Selection. *Recommendations for Improving Trustee Selection in Private Colleges & Universities.* Washington, D.C.: Association of Governing Boards of Universities and Colleges, 1980.

Phillips, David M. "Managerial Misuse of Property: The Synthesizing Thread in Corporate Doctrine." *Rutgers Law Review* 32 (July 1979): 184–236.

## ORIENTATION FOR NEW BOARD MEMBERS

American Bar Association, Committee on Corporate Laws, Section of Corporation, Banking, and Business Law. "Corporate Director's Guidebook." *Business Lawyer* 33 (April 1978): 1591–1644.

Ingram, Richard T. "Assuring Trustee Orientation and Development." In Ingram, op. cit., chap. 6.

Stitt, Susan. "Trusteeship Orientation: A Sound Investment." *Museum News* 59 (May/June 1981): 58 ff.

Young, Virginia G. *The Library Trustee: A Practical Guidebook.* New York: R. R. Bowker, 1969.

## BYLAWS AND RECORDS

Kolb, Charles E. M. "Delegation of Authority to Committees of the Board of Directors: Director's Liabilities." *University of Baltimore Law Review* 9 (Winter 1980): 189–216.

"Membership Rights in Nonprofit Corporations: A Need for Increased Legal Recognition and Protection." *Vanderbilt Law Review* 29 (April 1976): 747–75.

Oleck, Howard L. *Non-Profit Corporations, Organizations, and Associations.* 4th ed. Englewood Cliffs, N.J.: Prentice-Hall, 1980. Chapters 14 and 15 deal with minutes of meetings and bylaws.

―――. *Parliamentary Law for Nonprofit Organizations.* Philadelphia: ALI-ABA Committee on Continuing Professional Education, 1979.

## DISCLOSURE

"Statement on Conflicts of Interest." In Ingram, op. cit., app. D.

Willman, Frederick. "Written Guidelines on Conflicts of Interest." *Foundation News* 18 (May/June 1977): 51–54.

## ELECTION PROCEDURES

National Commission on College and University Trustee Selection. *Recommendations for Improving Trustee Selection in Private Colleges & Universities.* Washington, D.C.: Association of Governing Boards of Universities and Colleges, 1980.

## SELECTION OF CHAIRMAN AND OTHER OFFICERS

Connors, Tracy D. "Officers of the Nonprofit Organization." In Connors, op. cit., sec. 2, chap. 5.

## COMMITTEE STRUCTURE

Connors, Tracy D. "Committees of the Nonprofit Organization." In Connors, op. cit., sec. 2, chap. 6.

## FINANCE COMMITTEES

Choka, Allen D. "The New Role of the Audit Committee." *Practical Lawyer* 23 (September 1977): 53–60.

Clapp, Jane. *Professional Ethics and Insignia.* Metuchen, N.J.: Scarecrow Press, 1974. Pages 9–10 contain the code of the American Association of Certified Public Accountants, which requires that if accountants serve organizations in a professional capacity they should not be connected with the enterprise as a voting trustee or in any other managerial or employment capacity.

Groom, T. R., and Mazawey, L. T. "ERISA—Fiduciary Responsibility." In *Twenty-Eighth Annual Institute on Federal Taxation, University of Southern California Law Center,* pp. 973–1036. New York: Matthew Bender, 1976.

Little, H. Stennis, Jr., and Thrailkill, Larry T. "Fiduciaries under ERISA: A Narrow Path To Tread." *Vanderbilt Law Review* 30 (January 1977): 1–38.

Loo, Thomas S., and Feller, Lloyd H. "The Audit Committee." In *Ninth Annual Institute on Securities Regulation.* New York: PLI, 1978.

Middleditch, Leigh B., Jr. "Navigating for the Fiduciary Who Ships Out with the Not-For-Profit." *Ninth Annual Institute on Estate Planning, University of Miami Law Center,* chap. 9. New York: Matthew Bender, 1975.

*Stern v. Lucy Webb Hayes National Training School for Deaconesses and Missionaries,* 381 F. Supp. 1003 (D.D.C. 1974). The Sibley Hospital case, in which trustees were held to be responsible for conflicts of interest because board members were affiliated with institutions that did business with the hospital.

Uniform Management of Institutional Funds Act, section 5 (1972). A growing number of jurisdictions give the governing board of the institution the authority to delegate investment duties both within the organization and to outside experts.

## COLLECTIONS MANAGEMENT COMMITTEE

Association of Art Museum Directors. *Professional Practices in Art Museums.* Savannah, Ga.: AAMD, 1981. See pages 10–13.

Berger, Thomas J.; Neuner, A. M.; and Edwards, Stephen R. *Directory of Federally Controlled Species.* Lawrence, Kans.: Association of Systematics Collections, 1980.

Coggins, George Cameron, and Patti, Sebastion T. "The Emerging Law of Wildlife II: A Narrative Bibliography of Federal Wildlife Law." *Harvard Environmental Law Review* 4 (1980): 164–90.

———, and Smith, Deborah Lyndall. "The Emerging Law of Wildlife: A Narrative Bibliography." *Environmental Law* 6 (Winter 1976): 583–618.

*Harris v. Attorney General*, 31 Conn. Supp. 93, 324 A.2d 279, 287 (1974). The court determined that museum trustees have a duty, in providing security for the collection, "to exercise that care and prudence which an ordinarily prudent person would who was entrusted with the management of like property for another."

Hart, C. W., Jr. "The Burden of Regulation." *Museum News* 56 (January/February 1978): 23–25.

Merryman, John Henry, and Elsen, Albert E. *Law, Ethics and the Visual Arts.* New York: Matthew Bender, 1979. Sections 1 and 2 contain commentary and materials on the problems of theft and destruction of cultural patrimony.

Meyer, Karl E. *The Plundered Past.* New York: Atheneum, 1973.

Rodgers, David A., and Schaechter, N. Jack. "Environmental Law—The Survival of the Endangered Species Act." *1979 Annual Survey of American Law* (1979): 227–57.

Rosenberg, Ronald H. "Federal Protection of Unique Environmental Interests: Endangered and Threatened Species." *North Carolina Law Review* 58 (March 1980): 491–559.

Simmons, Robert M. "The Endangered Species Act of 1973." *South Dakota Law Review* 23 (Spring 1978): 302–25.

Stromberg, David B. "Endangered Species Act Amendments of 1978: A Step Backwards?" *Boston College Environmental Affairs Law Review* 7 (1978): 33–42.

———. "Endangered Species Act of 1973: Is the Statute Itself Endangered?" *Environmental Affairs* 6 (1978): 511–33.

## BUILDINGS AND GROUNDS COMMITTEE

Nelson, Charles A. "Managing Resources." In Ingram, op. cit., chap. 16. See especially pages 345–47.

## NOMINATING COMMITTEE

National Commission on College and University Trustee Selection. *Recommendations for Improving Trustee Selection in Private Colleges & Universities* and *Recommendations for Improving Trustee Selection in Public Colleges & Universities.* Washington, D.C.: Association of Governing Boards of Universities and Colleges, 1980.

## THE CHAIRMAN OF THE BOARD

Doyle, Michael, and Straus, David. *How To Make Meetings Work: The New Interaction Method.* Chicago: Playboy Press, 1976.

Stern, Alfred R. "Instilling Activism in Trustees." *Harvard Business Review* 58 (January/February 1980): 24–32. Discusses the chairman's role in motivating trustees.

## THE BOARD AND THE DIRECTOR

### SELECTING THE DIRECTOR

Jensen, Jerry. "Executive Pay: Deciding How Much Is Enough." *Grantsmanship Center News* 9 (January/February 1981): 28–35.

McQuade, Walter. "Management Problems Enter the Picture at Art Museums." In *Managing Nonprofit Organizations*, edited by Diane Borst and Patrick J. Montana, pp. 261–69. New York: AMACOM, 1977.

Nason, John W. "Selecting the Chief Executive." In Ingram, op. cit., chap. 8.

Naumer, Helmuth J. *Of Mutual Respect and Other Things: An Essay on Museum Trusteeship.* Washington, D.C.: AAM, 1977.

Shestack, Alan. "The Director: Scholar and Businessman, Educator and Lobbyist." *Museum News* 57 (November/December 1978): 27 ff.

### WORKING WITH THE DIRECTOR

See also the references cited for chapter II, section on Policy and Administration.

Rich, Daniel Catton. "Management, Power, and Integrity." In *On Understanding Art Museums*, edited by Sherman E. Lee, pp. 131–62. Englewood Cliffs, N.J.: Prentice-Hall, 1975.

### EVALUATING THE DIRECTOR

Munitz, Barry. "Reviewing Presidential Leadership." In Ingram, op. cit., chap. 19.

## THE BOARD AND THE STAFF

American Association of Museums, Committee on Ethics. *Museum Ethics.* Washington, D.C.: AAM, 1978. Pages 13, 23 and 30 contain statements concerning the trustees' obligations to respect the professionalism of the staff.

Nason, John W. *Trustees and the Future of Foundations.* New York: Council on Foundations, 1977. See pages 63–71.

# Chapter IV. Accountability of Museum Trustees

## ACCOUNTABILITY

See the references cited for chapter V, first general section.

## TO FELLOW TRUSTEES

"Capacity of Trustees of Charitable Corporations To Sue Co-Trustees To Enjoin Breach of Trust." *Hastings Law Journal* 16 (February 1965): 479–83.

*Holt v. College of Osteopathic Physicians and Surgeons,* 61 Cal. 2d 750, 394 P.2d 932, 40 Cal. Rptr. 244 (1964). The court determined that the power of the attorney general to bring suit is not exclusive.

Karst, Kenneth L. "The Efficiency of the Charitable Dollar: An Unfulfilled State Responsibility." *Harvard Law Review* 73 (January 1960): 433–83. Page 444 deals with instituting court proceedings against a trustee.

Restatement (Second) of Trusts, section 200 (1959). Deals with instituting court proceedings against a trustee.

*Richards v. Midkiff,* 48 Hawaii 32, 396 P.2d 49, 56 (1964). The court determined that a charitable trustee should institute litigation to prevent his cotrustee from committing a breach of trust or to compel him to redress such breach.

Scott, Austin W. *The Law of Trusts.* 3d ed. Boston: Little, Brown & Co., 1967. Section 200.2 discusses standing to sue a trustee.

## TO MEMBERS

"Membership Rights in Nonprofit Corporations: A Need for Increased Legal Recognition and Protection." *Vanderbilt Law Review* 29 (April 1976): 747–75.

*Wickes v. Belgian American Educational Foundation,* 226 F. Supp. 38 (S.D.N.Y. 1967). The court determined that members and directors of a charitable corporation have standing to sue to enjoin the unlawful conduct of the charitable corporation.

## TO STAFF

Glaser, Jane R. "Museum Studies: Suggested Qualifications for Museum Positions." *Museum News* 59 (October 1980): 26–31.

Westin, Alan F.; Kurtz, Henry I.; and Robbins, Albert. *Whistle Blowing! Loyalty and Dissent in the Corporation.* New York: McGraw-Hill, 1981. Presents studies of cases in which employees called management to account, with discussions and citations of the respective legal rights of management and staff.

Wilson, James A. "Management of Mental Health in Nonprofit Organizations." In Zaltman, op. cit., chap. 4. Presents a personnel management system that suggests increased accountability to employees' needs.

## TO DONORS

*Abrams v. Maryland Historical Society,* Circuit Court for Baltimore City, Equity No. A–58791; A–513/1979 (1979). The court upheld the right of a historical society to deaccession an object donated without formal restrictions on its disposal.

*Amato v. Metropolitan Museum of Art,* Supreme Court, New York County, Special Term Part I, Index No. 15122/79 (1979). The court determined that discretion is vested in the donee museum with respect to loan of donated objects.

DuBoff, Leonard D. *The Deskbook of Art Law.* Washington, D.C.: Federal Publications, 1977. See pages 921–24.

Feldman, Franklin, and Weil, Stephen E. *Art Works: Law, Policy, Practice.* New York: Practising Law Institute, 1974. See pages 1093–1111.

Fremont-Smith, Marion R. *Foundations and Government.* New York: Russell Sage Foundation, 1965. Pages 200–202 discuss the authorities supporting the general rule that the attorney general cannot be required to investigate or sue a charity.

McQuade, Walter. "Norton Simon's Great Museum Caper." *Fortune* 102 (August 25, 1980): 78–84. Describes the situation underlying *Rowan v. Pasadena Art Museum.*

Rosenbaum, Lee. "The Care and Feeding of Donors." *Art News* 77 (November 1978): 97–105.

*Rowan v. Pasadena Art Museum,* Superior Court, State of California, County of Los Angeles, No. C–322817 (May 15, 1980). Donors petitioned to attempt to stop the disposal of works of art by a museum, raising questions of the legal rights of donors to challenge deaccessioning. (See Memorandum order, June 30, 1981.)

## TO ARTISTS

Merryman, John H. "The Refrigerator of Bernard Buffet." *Hastings Law Journal* 27 (May 1976): 1023–49.

————, and Elsen, Albert E. *Law, Ethics and the Visual Arts.* New York: Matthew Bender, 1979. See section 4, pages 1–42.

Roeder, Martin A. "The Doctrine of Moral Right: A Study in the Law of Artists, Authors and Creators." *Harvard Law Review* 53 (February 1940): 554–78.

Weil, Stephen E. "The Moral Right Comes to California." *Art News* 78 (December 1979): 88–94.

## TO GROUPS WITH AN INTEREST IN MUSEUMS

American Association of Museums, Committee on Ethics. *Museum Ethics.* Washington, D.C.: AAM, 1978. See pages 13, 23 and 30.

Association of Art Museum Directors. *Professional Practices in Art Museums.* Rev. ed. Savannah, Ga.: AAMD, 1981.

Swinney, H. J., ed. *Professional Standards for Museum Accreditation.* Washington, D.C.: AAM, 1978.

## TO GROUPS CLAIMING CULTURAL PATRIMONY

Blair, Bowen. "American Indians vs. American Museums: A Matter of Religious Freedom—To Preserve Relics and Destroy Culture?" *American Indian Journal* 5 (May 1979): 13–21, and (June 1979): 2–6.

Capstick, Brenda, and Associates. "The Return and Restitution of Cultural Property: A Report." *Museums Journal* 79 (September 1979): 67–71.

Hill, Richard. "Reclaiming Cultural Artifacts." *Museum News* 55 (May/June 1977): 43–46.

Robinson, Alma. "The Art Repatriation Dilemma." *Museum News* 58 (March/April 1980): 55–59.

## TO THE PUBLIC AT LARGE

*Christiansen v. National Savings and Trust Co.,* U.S. District Court for the District of Columbia, Civil Action No. 70–1833, Memorandum order by Judge Harold H. Greene, October 16, 1980. The court limited the rights of members of the public to sue charities.

Hopkins, Bruce R. *The Law of Tax-Exempt Organizations.* 3d ed. New York: John Wiley & Sons, 1979. Section 38.7 deals with taxpayer standing to sue.

"Standing for Public and Quasi-Public Interest Tax Litigants." *Washington University Law Quarterly* (Summer 1978): 571–92.

## TO THE STATE AND THE COURTS

Abbott, Warren J., and Kornblum, Carole Ritts. "Jurisdiction of the Attorney-General over Corporate Fiduciaries under the New California Nonprofit Corporation Law." *University of San Francisco Law Review* 13 (Summer 1979): 753–96.

Edmisten, Rufus L. "The Common Law Powers of the Attorney General of North Carolina." *North Carolina Central Law Journal* 9 (Fall 1977): 1–36. Pages 23–29 deal with the enforcement of charitable trusts.

Fisch, Edith L.; Freed, Doris Jonas; and Schachter, Esther R. *Charities and Charitable Foundations.* Pomona, N.Y.: Lond Publications, 1974. Chapter 27 deals with supervision of charitable organizations.

Fremont-Smith, Marion R. "Duties and Powers of Charitable Fiduciaries: The Law of Trusts and the Correction of Abuses." *UCLA Law Review* 13 (May 1966): 1041–59.

————. *Foundations and Government.* New York: Russell Sage Foundation, 1965.

Friedman, Richard E. "State Administration of Charities." *Cleveland State Law Review* 19 (May 1970): 273–80.

Gray, Robert L. "State Attorney General—Guardian of Public Charities???" *Cleveland-Marshall Law Review* 14 (May 1965): 236–52. Summarizes the legislation of each state concerning the supervision of charitable trusts and nonprofit corporations.

Howland, Wallace. "History of the Supervision of Charitable Trusts and Corporations in California." *UCLA Law Review* 13 (May 1966): 1029–40.

Karst, Kenneth L. "The Efficiency of the Charitable Dollar: An Unfulfilled State Responsibility." *Harvard Law Review* 73 (January 1960): 433–83.

Kutner, Luis. *Legal Aspects of Charitable Trusts and Foundations: A Guide for Philanthropoids.* New York: Commerce Clearing House, Inc., 1970. Chapter 10 deals with state and federal regulation of charitable trusts.

Lane, Marc J. *Legal Handbook for Nonprofit Organizations.* New York: AMACOM, 1980. Chapter 9, "Charitable Fund Raising," discusses the range of charitable solicitation legislation.

Oleck, Howard L. *Non-Profit Corporations, Organizations, and Associations.* 4th ed. Englewood Cliffs, N.J.: Prentice-Hall, 1980. Chapters 30 and 31 deal with state taxes and exemptions.

————. *Trends in Nonprofit Organizations Law.* Philadelphia: ALI-ABA Committee on Continuing Professional Education, 1977. Page 47 explains that 33 states require annual reporting by charitable trusts and foundations.

"The Solicitor General and Intragovernmental Conflict." *Michigan Law Review* 76 (December 1977): 324–64. Page 334 begins a discussion of state attorney general powers.

"Sour Note on Sweet Charity: Is Attorney-General's Control Effective." *Lincoln Law Review* 9 (1974–75): 257–67.

## TO THE FEDERAL GOVERNMENT

Buratt, William D. "Completing and Filing Form 990: Accounting and Legal Issues and Determinations." *New York University Conference on Charitable Foundations* 10 (1971): 155–206.

Elder, Betty Doak, and Stone, John K. P. "Audit!" *History News* 35 (August 1980): 7–11. Discusses audits of museum shops.

Hopkins, Bruce R. *The Law of Tax-Exempt Organizations.* 3d ed. New York: John Wiley & Sons, 1979. Chapter 38 deals with the maintenance of tax-exempt status.

Leibowitz, E. K. "Officers' Personal Liability for Corporate Debts When Bankruptcy Ensues." *Commercial Law Journal* 82 (January 1977): 10–13.

Meyers, John. "Preparation of Forms 990 and 990–T." *Catholic Lawyer* 22 (Summer 1976): 256–61.

Spieller, William M. "The Favored Tax Treatment of Purchasers of Art." *Columbia Law Review* 80 (March 1980): 214–66. Sets forth proposals to limit the tax deductibility of gifts to museums.

Uniform Trustees' Powers Act, section 3(b). Imposes upon a trustee a duty not to exercise his powers "in such a way as to deprive the trust of an otherwise available tax exemption, deduction, or credit for tax purposes." See Utah Code Ann. (Supp. 1971), section 59–23–5.

United States Code, Title 18, sections 641 and 1001. Provide a basis for criminal prosecution where government funds are spent in an unauthorized manner or were obtained by some form of misrepresentation.

United States Treasury Regulation, section 301.6652–2 (1971). Deals with the failure by tax-exempt organizations and certain trusts and their managers, officers, directors or trustees to file certain returns or annual reports.

NOTE: Some states require trustees and managers of a private foundation to refrain from acting or to act in such a way as not to subject the foundation to federal excise taxes. See, e.g., S.C. Code (1976), section 21–31–60; Mich. Comp. Laws Ann. (Supp. 1980), section 14.275; Utah Code Ann. (Supp. 1971), section 59–23–5; Mo. Stat. Ann. (Supp. 1981), section 456.230. See also the discussion of the Connecticut legislation by J. Danford Anthony, Jr., "Private Foundation Governing Instrument Requirements: 1971 Connecticut Public Acts Nos. 219 and 220." *Connecticut Bar Journal* 46 (June 1972): 287–309.

## SPECIAL ACCOUNTABILITY OF THE GOVERNMENT MUSEUM

"Applying the Freedom of Information Act in the Area of Federal Grant Law: Exploring an Unknown Entity." *Cleveland State Law Review* 27 (1978): 294–311.

Moak, Lennox L., and Hillhouse, Albert M. *Concepts and Practices in Local Government Finance.* Chicago: Municipal Finance Officers Association, 1975.

Shurtz, Nancy E. "The University in the Sunshine: Application of the Open Meeting Laws to the University Setting." *Journal of Law and Education* 5 (October 1976): 453–64.

Simon, Arthur M. "The Application of State Sunshine Laws to Institutions of Higher Education." *Journal of College and University Law* 4 (Winter 1976–77): 82–145.

## RESPONDING TO INQUIRIES

Connors, Tracy D. "Public Information." In Connors, op. cit., sec. 5, chap. 2.

"Symposium: Openness in Government—A Continuing Era." *Federal Bar Journal* 38 (Fall 1979): 95–191.

# Chapter V. Liabilities of Museum Trustees

Aiken, Ray J. "Tort Liability of Governing Boards, Administrators and Faculty in Higher Education." *Journal of College and University Law* 2 (Winter 1975): 129–41.

Brown, Kristen M. "The Not-For-Profit Corporation Director: Legal Liabilities and Protection." *Federation of Insurance Counsel Quarterly* 28 (Fall 1977): 57–87.

Calfas, John A. "Boards of Directors: A New Standard of Care." *Loyola University Law Review (Los Angeles)* 9 (September 1976): 820–37.

Failing, Patricia. "Is the Norton Simon Museum Mismanaged?" *Art News* 79 (October 1980): 136–42. Describes *Rowan v. Pasadena Art Museum,* a legal action challenging the right of a museum to dispose of objects in its collections.

German, Edward C., and Gallagher, Michael D. "Liability of Corporate Officers and Directors: A Brief Survey of an Expanding Field." *Federation of Insurance Counsel Quarterly* 30 (Spring 1980): 187–204.

Hawkins, A. J. "Personal Liability of Charity Trustees." *Law Quarterly Review* 95 (January 1979): 99–116. Discusses the English law of trustee liability.

Knepper, William E. *Liability of Corporate Officers and Directors.* 3d ed. Indianapolis: Allen Smith Co., 1978. Chapter 9 deals with the liability of managers of nonprofit organizations.

Mace, Myles L. "Standards of Care for Trustees." *Harvard Business Review* 54 (January/February 1976): 14 ff.

McQuade, Walter. "Norton Simon's Great Museum Caper." *Fortune* 102 (August 25, 1980): 78–84. Describes the situation underlying *Rowan v. Pasadena Art Museum.*

Marsh, Gordon H. "Governance of Non-Profit Organizations: An Appropriate Standard of Conduct for Trustees and Directors of Museums and Other Cultural Institutions." *Dickinson Law Review* 85 (Summer 1981): 101–21. An experienced lawyer for museum trustees discusses theory, cases and practical considerations.

Merryman, John H. "Are Museum Trustees and the Law out of Step?" *Art News* 74 (November 1975): 24–27. Describes situations involving dereliction of duty by trustees.

Oleck, Howard L. "Nature of Nonprofit Organizations in 1979." *University of Toledo Law Review* 10 (Summer 1979): 962–84.

———. "Trends in Nonprofit Corporation Law in 1976." *Akron Law Review* 10 (Summer 1976): 71–91.

Perham, John C. "Nonprofit Boards under Fire." *Dun's Review* 114 (October 1979): 108–13.

Porth, William C. "Personal Liability of Trustees of Educational Institutions." *Journal of College and University Law* 2 (Winter 1975): 143–56.

"Report of the Committee on Charitable Trusts: Duties of Charitable Trust Trustees and Charitable Corporation Directors." *Real Property, Probate, and Trust Law Journal* 2 (Winter 1967): 545–64.

Restatement (Second) of Trusts, section 205(a) (1959). Trustee who commits a breach of trust is chargeable with any loss or depreciation in value of the trust estate resulting from the breach of trust.

*Rowan v. Pasadena Art Museum,* Superior Court, State of California, County of Los Angeles, California, No. C–322817 (May 15, 1980). A legal challenge to a museum's deaccessioning policies and practices. See the articles by Failing and McQuade, cited above.

Shaneyfelt, Donald L. "The Personal Liability Maze of Corporate Directors and Officers." *Nebraska Law Review* 58 (1979): 692–717.

Wakeling, Audrey A. "A Proposal To Limit the Civil Liability of Corporate Directors and Officers." *Insurance Law Journal* (October 1976): 608–21.

## LIABILITY FOR COLLECTIONS MANAGEMENT

*Abel v. Girard Trust Company,* 365 Pa. 34, 73 A.2d 682 (1950). The court determined that certain property held by a charity is in trust for the public. (See Pennsylvania Consolidated Statutes, Title 15, section 7549).

Carey, Ted. "Bringing Museum Ethics into Focus." *Art News* 77 (April 1978): 93–98.

———. "The Kan Case: Exploiting Museum Resources, or Faithful to His Duties?" *Art News* 77 (March 1978): 100–104. This article and the one by Carey cited above discuss the suit against a former curator of the Brooklyn Museum for alleged negligence in carrying out his fiduciary responsibilities to the collections and for allegedly defrauding the museum.

Failing, Patricia. "The Maryhill Museum: A Case History of Cultural Abuse." *Art News* 76 (March 1977): 83–90. Discusses neglect of the buildings and the collections by officers and trustees. (See *State ex rel. Gorton v. Leppaluoto* and the other lawsuits that arose in this museum.)

Fremont-Smith, Marion. *Foundations and Government.* New York: Russell Sage Foundation, 1965. Pages 130–32 discuss the concept that a nonprofit corporation holds property in trust for its public beneficiaries.

*Illinois Railway Museum v. Hansen,* 19th Judicial Circuit, McHenry County, Woodstock, Ill., No. 80 CH 229 (October 17, 1980). A suit against a former trustee to establish the museum's title in objects held and restored by the museum.

*In re Estate of Becker,* 270 Cal. App. 2d 31, 75 Cal. Rptr. 359, 362 (1969). The court determined that a charitable organization is the trustee of property it holds for charitable purposes.

*Lefkowitz ex rel. The Brooklyn Museum v. Kan,* Supreme Court, State and County of New York, No. 40082/78 (January 4, 1978). Suit against a former curator, a dealer, an appraiser and others, to recover over two million dollars in alleged damages to the museum and its collections for actions allegedly in violation of duties to the collections. This suit raises the legal issue whether fiduciary responsibility for the collections can be shifted from the trustees to a curator.

*Lefkowitz v. Museum of the American Indian—Heye Foundation,* Supreme Court, State and County of New York, No. 41416/75 (June 27, 1975). Petition by the attorney general alleging trustee misconduct and mismanagement with respect to the collections, resulting in a restraining order on dispositions. Also see the stipulation (August 27, 1975) wherein the museum agreed to cease any deaccessioning except upon permission of the attorney general, and to complete an inventory.

Lincoln, Alexander. "A Question on Gifts to Charitable Corporations." *Virginia Law Review* 25 (May 1939): 764–95.

*Parkinson v. Murdock*, 183 Kan. 706, 332 P.2d 273 (1958). The court determined that trustees of a charitable trust to provide an art collection for a city have a duty to properly house and care for the art objects purchased and to prevent their deterioration.

*People of the State of Illinois ex rel. William J. Scott, Attorney General v. Silverstein*, Circuit Court, Cook County, Ill., County Department, Chancery Division, No. 76 CH 6446 (October 28, 1976). Trustees of a museum were alleged to have the fiduciary responsibilities of common law trustees with respect to the collections and other assets and to be in violation of their obligations by mismanagement of collections and sales of museum objects to meet improperly incurred operating expenses.

*State of Washington ex rel. Slade Gorton v. Leppaluoto*, Superior Court, State of Washington, Klickitat County, No. 11781 (April 5, 1977). Petition by the attorney general against the former director and the present and former trustees of the museum alleging failure to protect, manage or maintain the museum's collections. This case was dismissed pursuant to a settlement agreement. See also the related case, No. 11777, *Maryhill Museum of Fine Arts v. Campbell*, Superior Court, State of Washington, Yakima County, No. 78–2–01952–7. A suit against the replacement director of the museum alleging that he mismanaged the collections. This suit was settled, with the concurrence of the attorney general, when the replacement director agreed to provide $10,000 for the museum's collections.

## LIABILITY FOR ACQUISITIONS

Berger, Thomas J.; Neuner, A. M.; and Edwards, Stephen R. *Directory of Federally Controlled Species*. Lawrence, Kans.: Association of Systematics Collections, 1980.

McAlee, James R. "The McClain Decision: A New Legal Wrinkle for Museums." *Museum News* 57 (July/August 1979): 29–33.

United States Code, Title 16, sections 470aa–470ll. The Archaeological Resources Protection Act of 1979.

*United States v. Molt*, 615 F.2d 141 (3d Cir. 1980). See also *United States v. Molt*, 599 F.2d 1217 (3d Cir. 1979). Prosecution against an importer of wildlife.

## LIABILITY FOR CONFLICTS OF INTEREST

Anderson, Alison Grey. "Conflicts of Interest: Efficiency, Fairness and Corporate Structure." *UCLA Law Review* 25 (April 1978): 738–95.

Bruce, William C. "Theft of Business Opportunity: The Legal Bases for a Claim against the Thief." *Connecticut Bar Journal* 53 (April 1979): 164–75.

Bulbulia, Ahmed, and Pinto, Arthur R. "Statutory Responses to Interested Directors' Transactions: A Watering Down of Fiduciary Standards?" *Notre Dame Lawyer* 53 (December 1977): 201–28.

"The Fairness Test of Corporate Contracts with Interested Directors." *Harvard Law Review* 61 (January 1948): 335–44.

*Matter of Estate of Rothko*, 43 N.Y.2d 305, 372 N.E.2d 291, 401 N.Y.S.2d 449 (1977). Conflicts of interest by executors of an estate, with resulting liability.

Seldes, Lee. *The Legacy of Mark Rothko*. New York: Holt, Rinehart, & Winston, 1978. A journalist's account of the conflicts of interest on the part of the executors of the Rothko estate.

"The Tests of Corporate Opportunity." *Cumberland Law Review* 8 (Winter 1978): 941–63.

## COLLECTING OBJECTS RELATED TO THE MUSEUM'S COLLECTIONS

*Hunter v. Shell Oil Co.*, 198 F.2d 485 (5th Cir. 1952). Employee was determined to be liable to the corporation for misuse of his position for personal advantage.

*Mile-o-Mo Fishing Club, Inc. v. Noble*, 62 Ill. App. 2d 50, 210 N.E.2d 12 (1965). An officer who took advantage of his position was ordered to reconvey property to the corporation.

*Mountain Top Youth Camp, Inc. v. Lyon*, 20 N.C. App. 694, 202 S.E.2d 498 (1974). A corporate officer improperly conveyed to himself land owned by the corporation.

Niles, Russell D. "Trustee Accountability in the Absence of Breach of Trust." *Columbia Law Review* 60 (January 1960): 141–60.

Scott, Austin W. *The Law of Trusts*. 3d ed. Boston: Little, Brown & Co., 1967. Section 504 states that it is improper for a fiduciary to purchase property sufficiently connected with the scope of his or her duties as a fiduciary.

*Valle v. North Jersey Automobile Club*, 310 A.2d 518 (1973). The court determined that officers were liable to the organization for profits improperly made because they took advantage of their positions in the organization.

## SELLING PRODUCTS AND SERVICES TO THE MUSEUM

"Corporate Counsel on the Board of Directors: An Overview." *Cumberland Law Review* 10 (Winter 1980): 791–831.

Knepper, William E. "Liability of Lawyer-Directors." *Ohio State Law Journal* 40 (1979): 341–60; also published in *Federation of Insurance Counsel Quarterly* 30 (Winter 1980): 161–83.

Mundheim, Robert H. "Should Code of Professional Responsibility Forbid Lawyers To Serve on Board of Corporation for Which They Act as Counsel." *Business Lawyer* 33 (March 1978): 1507–18.

Riger, Martin. "The Lawyer-Director—'A Vexing Problem.' " *Business Lawyer* 33 (July 1978): 2381–88.

"Should Lawyers Serve as Directors of Corporations for Which They Act as Counsel?" *Utah Law Review* (1978): 711–40.

"Trustees', Directors' and Attorneys' Fees for Services Rendered to Charitable Trusts and Corporations: What Is Reasonable?" *California Western Law Review* 16 (1980): 129–60.

Welles, Chris. "Nonprofit Institutions." In *Abuse on Wall Street: Conflicts of Interest in the Securities Markets*, edited by Roy Schotland, pp. 498–564. Westport, Conn.: Quorum Books, for the Twentieth Century Fund, 1980. Discusses the problems of interrelationships among trustees and those who manage the investments of nonprofit organizations.

## OTHER CONFLICTS OF INTEREST

*Conway v. Emeny*, 139 Conn. 612, 96 A.2d 221, 223 (1954). A trustee who was an officer of one organization voted to transfer its assets to another organization of which he was a trustee.

"Corporate Opportunity—Borden v. Sinsky: Strict Trust at Last?" *Journal of Corporate Law* 3 (Winter 1978): 422–35.

*Diamond v. Oreamuno*, 24 N.Y.2d 494, 248 N.E.2d 910, 301 N.Y.S.2d 78 (1969). The court determined that there can be liability for use of inside information even though the organization suffers no financial loss.

"Liability of Directors for Taking Corporate Opportunities, Using Corporate Facilities, or Engaging in a Competing Business." *Columbia Law Review* 39 (February 1939): 219–37.

*Matter of Estate of Rothko*, 43 N.Y.2d 305, 372 N.E. 2d 291, 401 N.Y.S.2d 449 (1977). The executors of an estate were removed for misconduct.

Phillips, David M. "Managerial Misuse of Property: The Synthesizing Thread in Corporate Doctrine." *Rutgers Law Review* 32 (July 1979): 184–236.

Scott, Austin W. *The Law of Trusts.* 3d ed. Boston: Little, Brown & Co., 1967. Section 203 deals with a trustee's accountability for profits made in the administration of a trust, even in the absence of a breach of trust.

Shreiber, Chanock, and Yoran, Aaron. "Allocation of Corporate Opportunities by Management." *Wayne Law Review* 23 (September 1977): 1355–72.

"The Tests of Corporate Opportunity." *Cumberland Law Review* 9 (Winter 1978): 941–63.

Treusch, Paul E., and Sugarman, Norman A. *Tax-Exempt Charitable Organizations.* Philadelphia : ALI-ABA Committee on Continuing Professional Education, 1979. Pages 32–34 discuss the limits of private inurement, with citation of authorities.

*Zehner v. Alexander,* Orphans' Court Division, Court of Common Pleas, 39th Judicial District Pa., Franklin County Branch, Decree of May 25, 1979. The court ordered a trustee of a college removed from the board because she was an executive officer of a similar institution and thus was found to have a conflict in her duties to the two institutions.

## PROTECTION FROM LIABILITY FOR CONFLICT OF INTEREST

Council of State Governments. *State Conflict of Interest/Financial Disclosure Legislation, 1972–75.* Lexington, Ky.: Council of State Governments, 1975. See the tables and summaries of the state laws.

*County of Nevada v. Macmillen,* 11 Cal. 3d 662, 522 P.2d 1345, 114 Cal. Rptr. 345 (1974). The court upheld the constitutionality of the California conflict of interest and financial disclosure laws covering individuals who serve as government officials.

"Fighting Conflicts of Interest in Officialdom: Constitutional and Practical Guidelines for State Financial Disclosure Laws." *Michigan Law Review* 73 (March 1975): 758–81.

Lascell, David M., and Hallenbeck, Alfred M. "Contending with Conflicts of Interest and Liability." In Ingram, op. cit., chap. 17.

Milrad, Aaron, and Agnew, Ella. *The Art World: Law, Business, & Practice in Canada.* Toronto: Merritt Publishing Co., 1980. See pages 74–75.

National Commission on College and University Trustee Selection. *Recommendations for Improving Trustee Selection in Private Colleges & Universities* and *Recommendations for Improving Trustee Selection in Public Colleges & Universities.* Washington, D.C.: Association of Governing Boards of Universities and Colleges, 1980. See appendix C, "Guidelines for Policies Affecting Potential Conflicts of Interest."

Schotland, Roy, ed. *Abuse on Wall Street: Conflicts of Interest in the Securities Markets.* Westport, Conn.: Quorum Books, for the Twentieth Century Fund, 1980. Pages 577–89 contain discussion and recommendations about disclosure procedures.

"Statement on Conflicts of Interest." In Ingram, op. cit., app. D. Includes suggested disclosure criteria and forms.

## FISCAL LIABILITIES

*Alperin v. United States,* U.S. District Court for the Western District of Tennessee, No. C–71–482 (December 2, 1971). The chairman of the board of a nonprofit theater was found personally liable for $16,000 plus interest and penalties because of theater's failure to pay over employee income taxes withheld, according to Internal Revenue Code, sections 6671 and 6672. Judgment was satisfied upon payment of $10,000 to the Internal Revenue Service.

Buratt, William D. "Completing and Filing Form 990: Accounting and Legal Issues and Determinations." *New York University Conference on Charitable Foundations* 10 (1971): 155–206.

Hopkins, Bruce R. *The Law of Tax-Exempt Organizations.* 3d ed. New York: John Wiley & Sons, 1979. Section 38.3 deals with the penalty imposed upon individuals who are responsible for a charitable organization's failure to file an information return.

Knepper, William E. "Liability of Corporate Officers for Debts of Financially Troubled Corporations." *Commercial Law Journal* 81 (October 1976): 389–95.

Leibowitz, E. K. "Officers' Personal Liability for Corporate Debts When Bankruptcy Ensues." *Commercial Law Journal* 82 (January 1977): 10–13.

Meyers, John. "Preparation of Forms 990 and 990–T." *Catholic Lawyer* 22 (Summer 1976): 256–61.

*People of the State of Illinois ex rel. William J. Scott, Attorney General v. Silverstein,* Circuit Court, Cook County, Ill., County Department, Chancery Division, No. 76 CH 6446 (October 28, 1976). The attorney general alleged self-dealing by museum trustees, including payment of excessive salaries to some trustees who served as officers.

*State of Washington ex rel. Slade Gorton v. Leppaluoto,* Superior Court, State of Washington, Klickitat County, No. 11781 (April 5, 1977). It was alleged that lax financial management by the trustees caused losses to the museum including its fiscal and real property resources.

United States Code, Title 26, sections 3403, 6671, 6672 and 7501. Provide the statutory basis for assertion of trustees' liability for employee income taxes withheld but not paid to the Internal Revenue Service.

United States Treasury Regulation, section 301.6652–2 (1971). Deals with the failure by tax-exempt organizations and certain trusts and their managers, officers, directors or trustees to file certain returns or annual reports.

## LIABILITY FOR NONMANAGEMENT

*Stern v. Lucy Webb Hayes National Training School for Deaconesses and Missionaries,* 381 F. Supp. 1003, 1014 (D.D.C. 1974). The court determined that a trustee of a nonprofit corporation may be personally liable for breach of fiduciary duty for the consistent failure to attend board meetings. A trustee may delegate responsibilities to fellow trustees but must exercise general supervision of their actions.

Stevenson, J. John. "A Case Study: Lessons in Board Responsibility." *Philanthropy Monthly* (October 1980): 25–27. Discusses a case of laxity in fiscal controls by trustees.

## CONSTITUTIONAL LIABILITIES

Brown, Kristen M. "The Not-For-Profit Corporation Director: Legal Liabilities and Protection." *Federation of Insurance Counsel Quarterly* 28 (Fall 1977): 57–87. Pages 72–74 deal with suits based on violations of constitutional rights that have been brought against not-for-profit corporations.

*Endress v. Brookdale Community College,* 144 N.J. Super. 109, 364 A.2d 1080 (1976). College president and trustees were found personally liable for the unconstitutional dismissal of a teacher.

Ewing, David W. "Civil Liberties in the Corporation." *New York State Bar Journal* 50 (April 1978): 188–91, 223–29.

———. *Freedom inside the Organization: Bringing Civil Liberties to the Workplace.* New York: Dutton, 1977.

"Free Speech and Impermissible Motive in the Dismissal of Public Employees." *Yale Law Journal* 89 (December 1979): 376–98.

O'Neil, Robert M. *The Rights of Government Employees.* New York: Avon Books, for the American Civil Liberties Union, 1978.

*Pickering v. Board of Education,* 391 U.S. 563 (1968). The court determined that speech by a public employee which entails a discussion of issues of public importance is protected.

Westin, Alan F., and Salisbury, Stephan, eds. *Individual Rights in the Corporation: A Reader on Employee Rights.* New York: Pantheon Books, 1980. See especially pages 156–74.

## LIABILITIES OF PENSION FUND TRUSTEES

Brown, Kristen M. "The Not-For-Profit Corporation Director: Legal Liabilities and Protection." *Federation of Insurance Counsel Quarterly* 28 (Fall 1977): 57–87. Pages 74–75 deal with responsibilities under ERISA.

Groom, T. R., and Mazawey, L. T. "ERISA—Fiduciary Responsibility." In *Twenty-Eighth Annual Institute on Federal Taxation, University of Southern California Law Center,* pp. 973–1036. New York: Matthew Bender, 1976.

Little, H. Stennis, Jr., and Thrailkill, Larry T. "Fiduciaries under ERISA: A Narrow Path To Tread." *Vanderbilt Law Review* 30 (January 1977): 1–38.

White, Geoffrey V. "Prudent Delegation of Trustees' Responsibilities to Professionals." *Labor Law Journal* 29 (September 1978): 586–93.

## INDEMNIFICATION AND INSURANCE PROTECTION

Brown, Kristen M. "The Not-For-Profit Corporation Director: Legal Liabilities and Protection." *Federation of Insurance Counsel Quarterly* 28 (Fall 1977): 57–87. Pages 75–87 deal with the protection of directors against the expenses of defending an action and a finding of liability.

Heyler, Groves R. "Indemnification of Corporate Agents." *UCLA Law Review* 23 (August 1976): 1255–68.

Hinsey, Joseph. "The New Lloyd's Policy Form for Directors and Officers Liability Insurance: An Analysis." *Business Lawyer* 33 (April 1978): 1961–92.

Johnston, Joseph F., Jr. "Corporate Indemnification and Liability Insurance for Directors and Officers." *Business Lawyer* 33 (April 1978): 1993–2053.

Knepper, William E. "An Overview of D & O Liability for Insurance Company Directors and Officers." *Insurance Counsel Journal* 45 (January 1978): 63–71.

Lane, Marc J. *Legal Handbook for Nonprofit Corporations.* New York: AMACOM, 1980. See pages 93–116.

Mattar, Edward Paul, III. "A Directors' and Trustees' Guide to Indemnification and Liability Insurance." *New York State Bar Journal* 51 (January 1979): 13; also published in *Commercial Law Journal* 83 (December 1978): 550–57.

Shaneyfelt, Donald L. "The Personal Liability Maze of Corporate Directors and Officers." *Nebraska Law Review* 58 (1979): 692–717.

Terrell, A. M., Jr. "Indemnification of Employees." *Delaware Journal of Corporate Law* 5 (1980): 251–75.

# Index

Abstention, 39, 79, 80, 85–86

Accountability of trustees, 2–3, 4, 62–72; for all board actions, 42, 43, 48; to artists, 65; to the courts (see also Courts), 4–5, 6, 67–69; to donors, 12, 17, 51, 64, 71–72; to the federal government (see also Grants, government; Internal Revenue Service; Regulatory laws; Withholding taxes), 69–70; to fellow trustees, 62–63; of government museums, 29–30, 44, 70–71, 88–89; to groups claiming cultural patrimony, 66; to groups with an interest in museums, 65–66; to members, 63; to the public at large, 5–6, 12, 27, 67, 72; to staff, 63–64; to the state (see also Attorneys general), 4–5, 6, 67–69

Accountants, 14, 49, 69; service on the board, 49. See also Conflicts of interest, selling products and services to the museum

Accounting, 25, 26–27. See also Audit

Accreditation, 13, 17, 66

Acquisitions, 11, 17, 18, 51, 64; of protected objects, materials and specimens (see also Cultural patrimony; Endangered species; UNESCO convention), 51, 66, 77–78; trustees' liability for, 77–78

Acquisitions committee. See Collections management committee

Administration: distinguished from policy (see also Director of the museum; Management), 9–10, 21–22, 28, 55, 58–60, 61, 88; trustees' responsibilities for, 10, 28–31

Advisory committees, 46

Advisory groups. See Support groups

Affiliate groups. See Support groups

Affirmative action regulations. See Nondiscrimination laws and regulations

Agendas, 33, 42, 55

American Association of Botanical Gardens and Arboreta, 66

American Association of Museums, 2, 65; accreditation program, 13, 17, 66

American Association for State and Local History, 65

American Association of Zoological Parks and Aquariums, 66

Appraisers, service on the board, 79. See also Conflicts of interest, selling products and services to the museum

"Art preservation" legislation. See Droit moral

Articles of incorporation. See Founding documents

Artists, trustees' accountability to, 65

Assessment. See Evaluation

Association, right of, 88

Association of Art Museum Directors, 65

Association of Science and Technology Centers, 65

Attorneys general: general oversight powers, 5, 6, 64, 67–69, 75–77, 86–87; powers regarding endowment and restricted funds, 25; powers regarding founding documents, 11; theories for trustees' accountability, 73

Audit, 25, 26–27, 49. See also Audit committee

Audit committee, 49

Bankers, service on the board, 26, 50–51. See also Conflicts of interest, selling products and services to the museum

Beneficence, 4

Board of trustees: administrative support, 43, 50, 58; composition, 9, 35–40, 45, 79; and the director (see also Administration, distinguished from policy), 9, 28–29, 32, 41, 55–61; functioning as a collective, 33, 35, 36–37, 54–55; officers (see also offi-

transfer of the collections, 12; use of proceeds, 18, 19, 76
Dealers: and deaccessioning, 19; service on the board, 38, 79. See also Conflicts of interest, selling products and services to the museum
Deeds of gift, 64
Deferred giving, 23
Development. See Fund raising
Development committee. See Fundraising committee
Development officer, 23, 50
Director of the museum, 28–29, 55–61; accountability for compliance with regulatory laws, 69; acting, 22; and the board of trustees (see also Administration, distinguished from policy), 9, 28–29, 32, 41, 55–61; and the chairman of the board, 45, 54, 55, 60; employment agreements, 58, 60; evaluation, 32–33, 58, 60–61; job description, 28–29, 56, 60; qualifications, 56; reporting to the board, 32, 59; responsibilities for the collections, 16, 17, 18, 75–76, 86; responsibilities for financial management, 13, 21–22, 23, 26, 27, 32; responsibilities for museum operations, 28, 55; responsibilities for personnel matters, 21–22, 28, 31, 53, 61; selection, 28, 55–59; and selection of trustees, 35; termination, 58, 60; as a trustee, 58–59. See also Staff
Disclosure: bylaws relating to, 42, 44; of museum records, 70, 71–72, 85; as protection from conflict of interest, 26, 50–51, 79, 80, 82, 84, 85; statements, 26, 42, 44, 80, 85, 88
Disclosure laws. See Public disclosure laws
Discrimination. See Nondiscrimination laws and regulations
Dissent, 43, 48, 63, 75, 89
Donors, 13, 17, 23, 27, 64; income tax reduction advantages for, 14, 37, 69; trustees' accountability to, 12, 17, 51, 64, 71–72
Droit moral, 65
Due process, right of, 29–30

Education committee, 9–10, 53
Education policy, 20–21. See also Education committee
Employee Retirement Income Security Act (ERISA), 49, 90. See also Pension funds

Endangered species, 51, 77–78
Endowments, 11, 25, 49. See also Investment management
Equal employment opportunity regulations, 32, 56. See also Nondiscrimination laws and regulations
Ethics, code of, for AAM members, 66
Evaluation: of the board, 33; of the director, 32–33, 58, 60–61; of exhibitions, 32; of museum operations, 10, 31–33, 53, 56, 60–61
Executive committee, 35, 45, 46, 48–49, 71
Executive sessions, 43, 44, 58
Exhibitions: evaluation, 32; policy, 20, 38; standards, 19, 65, 66. See also Exhibitions committee
Exhibitions committee, 9–10, 51
Expenses, reimbursement for: candidates for directorship, 57; trustees, 57, 90. See also Indemnification; Insurance

Federal government, trustees' accountability to, 69–70. See also Grants, government; Internal Revenue Service; Nondiscrimination laws and regulations; Regulatory laws; Withholding taxes
Fiduciary: defined, 3, 4, 6; standards, 6, 74–75, 77, 79–80, 82, 83, 90
Finance committees, 25, 26, 45, 49–51. See also committees by name; Treasurer of the board
Financial management, 21–28; policy, 13–15, 21–28; trustees' liability for, 25, 86–87. See also Accounting; Audit; Budget; Cash management; Director, responsibilities for financial management; Finance committees; Fund raising; Investment management; Long-range planning
Financial planning. See Budget; Long-range planning
Financial reports, 27, 69
Fire codes, 16
Founding documents, 41, 90–91; amending, 11–12, 46–47; availability, 11, 40; in membership organizations, 41, 44–45, 46–47; as organization's statement of purpose, 10–12; security, 43
Freedom of information laws, 70, 72
Freedom of speech, right of, 29–30; trustees' liability for infringement of, 88–90

Fund raising, 13, 22–25, 28, 50, 64, 68–69. *See also* Development officer; Fund-raising committee
Fund-raising committee, 9–10, 22–23, 50, 53–54

Government museums, 27–28, 70–71; accountability of, 29–30, 44, 70–71, 85, 88–89; buildings and grounds committee, 52; constitutional rights of employees, 29–30, 88–90; financial regulations, 71; financial support, 27–28; freedom of information laws, 70, 72; governance, 2, 6, 40; "sunshine" laws, 44, 70–71
Governments. *See* Federal government; Local governments; State governments
Grantors, 13, 27, 32
Grants, 23–25, 32, 50; government grants, and compliance with regulatory laws, 1, 15–16, 69–70; misapplication of funds, 24, 70; obligations of the recipients, 24–25; procedures for accepting, 24–25, 50, 69–70
Grievance procedures, 30–31, 53

Handicapped access, 15, 32, 52. *See also* Nondiscrimination laws and regulations
Health and safety regulations, 16, 52, 69
Health and safety rights, 30

Indemnification, 44, 78, 90–92
Inquiries, responding to, 67, 70, 71–72
Inside information, use of, 19, 81, 83
Insurance, 49, 90–92; for buildings and grounds, 52; for the collections, 17–18, 52; for director and senior staff, 91; for libel, 91–92; for pension fund trustees, 90, 91, 92; for trustees, 44, 78, 90–92. *See also* Indemnification; Workmen's compensation
Internal Revenue Service, 10–11, 14, 16, 69, 87
International Council of Museums, 65
Investment committee, 49, 53–54
Investment management, 25–26, 49. *See also* Investment committee
Investment managers, 26, 49; service on the board, 26, 83. *See also* Conflicts of interest, selling products and services to the museum

Law, 4; developments in, 54; English common law, 4–6, 68. *See also* Attorneys general; Courts; *Droit moral;*
Legal rights; Regulatory laws; *other laws by name*
Law and planning committee, 54
Lawyers: Fees and costs, 67, 78, 88, 89, 91–92; service on the board, 82–83. *See also* Conflicts of interest, selling products and services to the museum; Legal counsel
Legal actions involving trustees, 73–77, 86–87, 88, 89–90; suits attempting to impose personal liability distinguished from suits against museums, 74
Legal counsel: on amending founding documents, 11; on conflicts of interest, 79, 83; for constitutional rights questions, 30; on disclosure of records, 72; on drafting bylaws, 41, 44, 70–71; on endowments and restricted funds, 25; on grievance procedures, 31, 53; on liabilities, 73; on pension funds, 90; on probation and/or dismissal of the director, 60; on tax-exempt status, 14
Legal rights: of the board, 60; of the director, 60; of employees, 29–30, 53, 88–90. *See also* Civil rights; Constitutional rights
Liabilities of trustees, 2–3, 3–4, 42–43, 62, 64, 69–70, 73–92; for acquisitions, 77–78; for collections management, 74–78, 86; for conflicts of interest, 78–84; defined, 73–74; for financial management, 25, 86–87; for infringement of constitutional rights, 30, 88–90; for nonmanagement, 88; for pension funds, 90; protection from (*see also* Conflicts of interest, protection from), 43, 63, 73, 85–86, 90–92
Libel, insurance for, 91, 92
Loans: policy, 17, 20, 51; procedures for approving, 51. *See also* Loans committee
Loans committee, 51. *See also* Exhibitions committee
Lobbying, 15
Local governments: bond issues for museums, 23; tax exemptions for museums, 14. *See also* Government museums
Long-range planning, 13, 22, 53–54. *See also* Planning committee

Management, 1, 13; standards for, 63–64, 65, 66, 88; subject to intervention by the state and the courts, 6, 67, 68, 74–75. *See also* Administration; Director of the museum; Non-management

Meetings: agenda, 33, 42, 55; attendance, 42–43, 54, 58; bylaws, 42–44; emergency, 42, 71; executive sessions, 43, 44, 58; open meeting ("sunshine") laws, 44, 70–71; procedures, 54–55, 59; scheduling, 33, 42–43, 45, 55, 60

Members: of membership organizations, 27, 41, 46, 63; of support groups, 63; trustees' accountability to, 63. See also Membership organizations; Support groups

Membership organizations, 27, 45, 46; election of trustees, 35, 46, 63; founding documents, 41, 44–45, 46–47; rights of members, 27, 63

Minimum wage regulations, 16, 68–69

Minutes, 43–44, 55; availability, 40, 55; recording dissent in, 43, 48; security, 43, 55. See also Records

Model Nonprofit Corporation Act, 6

*Museum Ethics,* 66

Museum libraries, 40, 51–52, 53

Museum shops, 14–15, 22

Museums: commercial activities of, 14–15, 22; as cultural centers, 1, 20–21, 22; defined, 2–3, 12, 13–14; groups with an interest in (see also *organizations by name*), 62, 65–66; heightened public awareness of, 1, 26, 62, 67; political activities of, 15. See also Government museums; Nonprofit corporations; Public charities

Nominating committee, 35, 39, 46, 52–53, 79

Nondiscrimination laws and regulations, 29–30, 68; compliance with in accepting government grants, 15–16, 70; compliance with in hiring the director, 56, 58; evaluation of the museum's compliance with, 32, 53

Nonmanagement, trustees' liability for, 88

Nonprofit corporations, 1, 11, 14–15, 26, 69; defined, 5–6, 13–14, 87

Officers of the board, 45. See also *officers by title*

Orientation of trustees, 40–41, 52–53; information about the museum, 11, 40; tour of facilities, 19–20, 40–41

Outreach committee. See Education committee

Pension fund committee, 49–50; insurance for, 90, 91, 92

Pension funds, 49–50; insurance for trustees, 90, 91, 92; trustees' liability for, 90. See also Pension fund committee

Personnel: appointment of staff, 22; authorization of positions, 21–22, 49. See also Personnel committee; Personnel policies; Staff

Personnel committee, 31, 53

Personnel policies, 29–31, 32; grievance procedures, 30–31, 53; legal rights of employees, 29–30, 53, 88–90

Physical plant. See Buildings and grounds

Planning. See Budget; Law, development in; Long-range planning

Planning committee, 53–54

Pluralism, 6

Policy: distinguished from administration, 9–10, 21–22, 28, 55, 58–60, 61, 88; distinguished from personal opinion, 9, 61

Policy making, 8–21, 54; general goals and purposes, 8–12, 22; policy statements, 10–12, 40, 41, 42; specific policies, 12–21. See also Long-range planning; Regulatory laws; Tax-exempt status; *other policies by name*

Political activities of museums, 15

Position, abuse of, 61, 84

President, 45. See also Chairman of the board

Private foundations, 14, 87

Private operating foundations, 14, 87

*Professional Standards for Museum Accreditation,* 66

Provenance, 66

Public access, 20–21

Public at large, trustees' accountability to, 5–6, 12, 27, 62, 67, 72

Public charities, 5, 6, 67–69; defined, 2, 5, 14, 63. See also Charitable trusts; Private operating foundations

Public disclosure laws, 72, 85

Public relations, 13, 28, 31–32, 53, 61, 67, 71–72. See also Public relations committee

Public relations committee, 53, 71

Records, 41–47, 55; disclosure, 70, 71–72, 85. See also *records by name*

Regulatory laws, compliance with, 1, 15–16, 51, 54, 68–69, 77–78. See also *laws by name*

Reports: annual, 67–68; committee, 42, 46, 48, 49; financial, 27, 69
Research policy, 20
Resolutions, 11, 40, 41, 42, 43
Responsibilities of trustees, 3, 8–33, 62, 63, 66, 88. *See also* Administration, trustees' responsibilities for; Evaluation; Financial management; Policy making
Restricted funds. *See* Endowments
Review. *See* Evaluation.

Safety regulations. *See* Health and safety regulations
Search committee, 56–57
Secretary, recording, 43–44
Secretary of the board, 43–44, 45, 55
Security for museums, 18, 19–20, 52
Selection of trustees, 35–40, 44–45, 52–53; consideration of potential conflicts of interest in, 37–39, 44, 79, 85. *See also* Nominating committee
Seminars and workshops, 13, 23, 33
Social security regulations, 16
Staff: and conflicts of interest, 19, 80–81; professionalism, 29, 61, 63–64; relations with trustees (*see also* Administration, distinguished from policy), 9–10, 29–31, 41, 61, 63–64; training, 29; trustees' accountability to, 63–64. *See also* Director of the museum; Personnel
Standing to sue, 67; artists', 64; donors', 64; other individuals', 5, 67, 88
State governments: tax exemptions for museums, 14; trustees' accountability to, 67–69. *See also* Attorneys general; Government museums
Statements of purpose, 10–12, 41, 42
Statute of Charitable Uses (1601), 4–5
"Sunshine" laws, 44, 70–71
Suppliers, service on the board, 37, 81–83. *See also* Conflicts of interest, selling products and services to the museum
Support groups, 22, 23, 35, 36, 39, 63

Tax-exempt status, 13–15, 69, 84; application for, 10, 14; most favorable, 14, 69; threats to, 14–15, 84
Tax exemptions, 14
Treasurer of the board, 45, 50
Trustees: accountability to other members of the board, 62–63; defined, 3–4; duty of loyalty, 3, 26, 37–39, 50–51, 63, 73–88, 90; *ex officio*, 39–40; historical precedents, 4–6; honorifics, 39; in non–common law countries, 6; opportunities, 7, 39, 92; relations with the director (*see also* Administration, distinguished from policy), 9, 28–29, 32, 41, 55–61; relations with staff, 9–10, 29–31, 41, 61, 63–64; standard of care, 3, 6, 73–77, 90; terms of service, 45; visibility (*see also* Museums, heightened public awareness of), 1, 2–3; as volunteers, 10, 23, 24, 50. *See also* Accountability of trustees; Board of trustees; Liabilities of trustees; Orientation of trustees; Responsibilities of trustees; Selection of trustees

UNESCO convention, 77
Union contracts, 29, 30, 53
Unrelated income, 15

Vice-chairman of the board, 45
Volunteers, 29, 53, 61; trustees as, 10, 23, 24, 50
Voting. *See* Abstention; Dissent

Withholding taxes, 16, 69, 87
Workmen's compensation regulations, 16
Workshops. *See* Seminars and workshops